Anita Di

PATTERNS
OF
PROPHECY

PATTERNS
OF
PROPHECY

by Alan Vaughan

HAWTHORN BOOKS, INC.
Publishers/NEW YORK

PATTERNS OF PROPHECY

1 2 3 4 5 6 7 8 9 10

To

Charles Fort, who doubted.
Hayes Jacobs, who believed.
Eileen Garrett, who trusted.
Iris Vaughan, who helped.

Contents

Foreword

Discussions on the nature of time have often centered around whether it exists as an independent thing (as a specific temporal entity) or whether it exists as a relationship between events (as an attribute of other things). These points of view mark the typical discourse on the absolute versus the relative nature of time.

Other discussions have centered around the objective, physical nature of time versus time's subjective, psychological nature. Within these frameworks, some writers have put forth the position that time is a reality while others have argued that it merely has the appearance of reality.

The physicist M. N. McMorris, in a provocative essay appearing in *Main Currents in Modern Thought* (Volume 29, 1973), notes how differently time can be conceived. To some, time appears to partake of the "static temporal" while to others it partakes of the "dynamic temporal." In the former instance, events are regarded to be simultaneously given in time in a serial, static order. In this case, the relevant relationship is "before" or "after." In the latter instance, events emerge in time and exhibit a flux as they go from the future through the present and into the past. This is a conceptualization of time as "becoming" rather than "being."

McMorris places Albert Einstein in this latter category and notes that the relativity of simultaneity concerns itself with separated events. It implies that the measured time between two such events may be different for two observers in relative motion. In particular, two events simultaneous for the one observer will not be simultaneous for the other. Such observers will certainly disagree among themselves as to the nature of the "present." For these observers the comprehensive order of "before and after" is impaired. The idea of time as an absolute for them is untenable. As T. S. Eliot wrote in "Burnt Norton,"

> Time present and time past
> Are both perhaps present in time future,
> And time future contained in time past
> If all time is eternally present.

This point of view is helpful to some in presenting a perspective on the topic of precognition. One person may be baffled by a dream about a future event or a prediction by a "psychic sensitive." However, to another observer the events may not appear to occupy different points in time. Indeed, many individuals who make precognitive statements have episodes in their lives in which they experience time as "eternally present"; this subjective feeling may be an important concomitant of their prophetic abilities.

Time may well be the most enigmatic property of nature. For Ludwig Feuerbach, the nineteenth-century philosopher, time was the very "cornerstone of being." J. B. Priestley, the essayist, has referred to precognitive dreams as "glimpses of a future already shaped but still pliable. . . ." H. H. Price, the philosopher, has stated that precognitive phenomena do occur, and that

> the universe might be a neater or tidier place if they did
> not, and human personality might also be a neater and tidier

thing. But we must put up with the facts as best we may; and if we have any philosophical curiosity, we must consider the bearing which they have on our theories of human personality.

During my visits to the U.S.S.R., I learned about the experiments with gyroscopes and pendulums by the Soviet astronomer Nikolai Kozyrev. It is known that if a weight or a balance beam is suspended elastically and if the base of the balance is vibrated, the weight can be observed to get heavier in proportion to its mass. Kozyrev has found that the weight measures the horizontal component of time flow forces caused by the earth's rotation, while the balance measures its vertical component. These experiments have produced results that suggest that time not only appears to flow but also has density. Furthermore, it seems time density is affected by processes at work in the terrestrial atmosphere, because the effects are observed more easily during the winter than in summer. Finally, the density seems to be "stretched" by cause and "compressed" by effect. Kozyrev has conjectured that his findings may someday help to explain such enigmatic psychic processes as precognition and telepathy.

Alan Vaughan is ideally equipped to discuss the patterns of prophecy, being a "psychic sensitive" with a distinguished career in science writing. I first met Mr. Vaughan at a 1967 conference in southern France sponsored by the Parapsychology Foundation. Readers of this book will find provocative Mr. Vaughan's account of synchronicity, of historical archetypes (one can almost see the Watergate affair step from the pages of ancient Greek drama), of his own remarkable predictions, and (unlike many celebrated prophets) his precognitive hunches that missed the mark.

As for myself, I find it obvious that people have many unusual experiences with time—perhaps more than they realize. I feel that some events in our lives are causal while

others are acausal. Thus, cause-and-effect as well as synchronicity must be accounted for by science as well as by
the individual who wants to live life fully. As T. S. Eliot
wrote, "There the dance is . . . , where past and future are
gathered. . . . Except for the point, the still point, there
would be no dance, and there is only the dance. . . ."

STANLEY KRIPPNER, PH.D.

PATTERNS
OF
PROPHECY

1

Why Prophecy?

This book started as a compulsion. I had to find out if prophecy was a reality or if I was losing my mind. The compulsion was triggered by events that began in 1965 when I was a twenty-eight-year-old science editor for a college textbook firm. I was a skeptic about psychic phenomena. I had never been aware of ever having a psychic experience. The scientific facts and theories of my textbooks fit neatly together, a tidy universe of knowledge that did not allow for the unexplainable. But the unexplainable seemed to seek me out.

It began on November 7, 1965, when I was trying out a newly purchased Ouija board to amuse a friend convalescing from an operation. Neither of us knew much about Ouijas except the notion that information spelled out on the board must come from our unconscious. Or so we thought. It told us that New York, where we were living, would be flooded in 1973. That seemed ridiculous. Then a radio newscast interrupted with the news that the columnist Dorothy Kilgallen had died of a heart attack. We asked the Ouija if this was true. No, it said, she had died by poison. Ten days later it was revealed by the newspapers that she had indeed died of poisoning—a combination of alcohol and barbiturates. At that point I became fascinated with the possibilities offered by the Ouija and began experimenting with it with a number of friends. "Spirits" began to appear on the board. One, who called himself "Z," answered our questions accurately and with a peculiarly old-fashioned vocabulary.

Later, I began to experiment alone with the Ouija and soon found myself "possessed" by a rather neurotic personality who called herself "Nada." "She" said on the board that she had lived in Nantucket and had a daughter, living, named Caxton (which I presumed was a married surname). But then, both to my fascination and fear, "Nada" got inside my head. I could hear her voice repeating the same phrases over and over again. "She" seemed to be jealous that I was living while she was only a "spirit." I took my Ouija to visit a friend to investigate further what was happening. I felt the presence of "Z" and across the room my friend announced that the pointer was starting to move. It went to "Z" and then spelled out a message: "Awful consequences—possession." At that point I became alarmed, for it had not occurred to me that having a strange voice in one's head was tantamount to possession.

We went then to see another friend to work the board in hopes of finding out how I could become "dispossessed." The board spelled out only gibberish, and I became increasingly frustrated. Suddenly, in addition to "Nada" in my head, I felt again the presence of "Z," who made me write out a message by hand: "Each of us has a spirit while living. Do not meddle with the spirits of the dead."

As I wrote out this message, I began to feel an energy rising up within my body and entering my brain. It pushed out both "Nada" and "Z." My friends noted that my face, which had been white and pinched, suddenly flooded with color. I felt a tremendous sense of elation and physical well-being. The energy grew stronger and seemed to extend beyond my body. My mind seemed to race in some extended dimension that knew no confines of time or space. For the first time, I began to sense what was going on in other people's minds and—to my astonishment—I began to sense the future through some kind of extended awareness. My first act in this strange but exciting state was to throw the Ouija board down an incinerator chute. Thus ended my investigation of the Ouija.

The immediate effect of that whole bizarre experience was the most extreme fright I had ever felt in my life. All the strange tales of the supernatural that I had formerly dismissed as foolish notions now took on a threatening possibility of reality. The gates of hell seemed to have been opened, and I trembled through two sleepless days and nights, wondering if anything else would happen. On Monday morning, in a near state of exhaustion, I telephoned my boss with what must have sounded like a rather strange excuse for absence: "I had been possessed by a spirit." To my surprise, he was sympathetic and mentioned that it reminded him of the dybbuk in Jewish folklore. That didn't exactly calm me, but it did make me curious if such experiences had happened to other people.

While there seemed to be no way to prove conclusively whether or not there might actually have been such a person as Nada—since I did not know enough about her life—yet the other strange phenomena that followed the apparent possession seemed verifiable, if not explainable. In one instance, on a Sunday morning while I was reading *The New York Times*, I felt a deep depression come over me for no apparent reason. I paused and tried to reason it out. But when I returned to reading about the scheduled launch of the *Gemini VI* spacecraft, the depression grew greater. Then I realized that something must be wrong with the *Gemini VI* that could cause disaster. I told a number of friends about this foreboding but felt helpless to prevent any disaster since I did not know exactly what was wrong with the spaceship. Fortunately, the

Gemini VI space launch was postponed after a misfire of some electrical switch. When the technicians checked over the ship again, they found a plastic cap in a fuel line—and fined the manufacturer $25,000 for this blundering oversight that could have caused disaster. Later, the ship was launched without mishap.

The next day I searched through a small bookshop next door to where I worked and found an oddly titled two-volume set of books that was marked down from $15.00 to $5.95: *Human Personality and Its Survival of Bodily Death* by Frederic W. H. Myers. It seemed like a good bargain so I bought it and began my exploration of parapsychology. Only much later did I discover that Myers's book, published posthumously in 1903, was the very cornerstone of psychical research and that I could not have begun my education in a better way.

Yet, as I studied this book and every other book on psychical research I could get my hands on, I could not find a single case of an absolutely established prophecy that was fulfilled. There were literally thousands of dreams that turned out, the dreamers said, to correspond to later events. Yet the dreamers had not written out their dreams at the time they happened but would say years later that their dreams had been "fulfilled in every detail."

A typical example was "Mrs. C's Monkey Dream." In 1867 she told her family that she had a dream in which a monkey was following her, which was distressing since she had a particular aversion from monkeys. Her husband advised her to go for a walk in their fashionable London neighborhood to dispel the menacing dream. Walking with her children, she passed the home of the Duchess of Argyll and saw a monkey on the roof of the coach house. The monkey began to follow her along the top of the wall, and she experienced again the terror of her dream. Later, she found out that the monkey was the Duchess's pet, which had escaped.

Twenty-one years later, in 1888, Mrs. C wrote to Myers with details of her story; he then received corroborative accounts from her husband and nurse and confirmed that there had been a monkey at Argyll Lodge twenty years before. Myers published the case in 1895—a lapse of twenty-eight years since it happened. How could anyone else verify this case?

As Fraser Nicol, one of the most critical psychical researchers to study precognition, has said: "One wonders whether several of these cases deserve the supreme place accorded them?"

I turned to books on prophecy at the New York Public Library in the hope that I might find the "magic prophetic list," a series of prophecies in print that could be documented in their fulfillment years later. Weeks of research grew into months as I methodically went through every book on prophecy at the library. I noticed a familiar pattern that made me suspicious. Like the magic staff of Moses, the publication dates of the books struck in twain the prophets' accuracy: prophecies "fulfilled" before the books' publication were all "accurate"; yet the prophets' "unerring" accuracy did not seem to hold up for events forecast *after* the books' publication.

I wrote a letter to Allan Angoff, a librarian and consultant at the Parapsychology Foundation in New York, asking if he knew of any special library collections on prophecy or any experts on the subject. Yes, he replied, a friend named Eileen Garrett has a good library on psychical research and she had written a book on prophecy (*The Sense and Nonsense of Prophecy*). Mr. Angoff invited me to have lunch with him and Mrs. Garrett to discuss my research. We dined at the Baroque, a fashionable Upper East Side restaurant that was a favorite of Mrs. Garrett's, and after three martinis we relaxed into earnest conversation. I listened in fascination to

Mrs. Garrett's stories about psychical research. She had started Tim Leary on an LSD-ESP project at Harvard, but he got carried away with the psychedelic part of it and never did write up his experiment. She got Aldous Huxley interested in ESP, and he had frequently visited her at her summer home in the South of France. She had published Robert Graves's book *The White Goddess* and featured writings by Graves and other literary celebrities in her magazine *Tomorrow*, the title of which she used again in starting a new magazine on psychical research. And, of course, she had one of the finest libraries in the world on parapsychology at the Parapsychology Foundation, which she had established in 1955. She invited me to use it for further research.

So I went through all the books there as well as the periodicals in search of fulfilled prophecy. Again, frustration. Mrs. Garrett invited me to lunch again and asked me how things were going.

"I'm afraid I've reached an impasse," I told her. "I can go no further with books. I must find people who can prophesy."

"Then I suppose I'll have to give you a grant," she casually replied. I quickly learned that by that statement she was prepared not only to finance a European research odyssey into prophecy for me and my wife, but also to plan the very moves I must make, the people I must see, the tasks I must do.

The first stop of my odyssey was in the South of France for a conference on LSD and ESP in June 1967. The conference, sponsored by the Parapsychology Foundation, provided a fascinating introduction to experimental parapsychology as well as early attempts to induce psychic ability with LSD. (LSD was not particularly helpful, it was concluded, unless a person already had developed his psychic ability.)

Among the conference participants was Fraser Nicol, the remarkable Scot whose prodigious research into the history of psychical research knew no peer. (He confessed he felt slightly out of place at an LSD conference since he had never take a pill in his life—not even an aspirin.)

Mr. Nicol had worked for the Society for Psychical Research in England and at the American Society for Psychical Research, J. B. Rhine's Parapsychology Laboratory, and the Parapsychology Foundation in the United States, where he resides now. Mr. Nicol has the most comprehensive grasp of the history and methodology of psychical research I have ever encountered; he also knows more about the scandals of psychical research than anyone else. In our long talks there and later in London, he documented in great detail the misfortunes that had befallen psychical researchers who had risked their reputations by publishing evidence for ESP that no one else could verify. Their critics frequently took the view that ESP is impossible, therefore the researchers must be fraudulent or duped. Both J. B. Rhine and Dr. S. G. Soal of England had been attacked on these grounds. Even the illustrious physicist Sir William Crookes had been accused of sleeping with his female medium who produced materializations. Hardly a researcher in parapsychology had gone without attacks on his personal integrity and reputation.

Taking Mr. Nicol's tales to heart, I decided to make as a criterion of prophecy the important rule that anyone must be able to verify a prophecy; that way no one person's reputation would be risked by my research. In practice, this meant that the prophecy must be recorded in print or registered with an organization before the event and that the fulfillment must be public knowledge of sufficient importance that it is recorded in newspapers or films.

The other criteria for prophecy (or foreknowledge, as it was termed by the British researcher H. F. Saltmarsh) were summarized by Mr. Nicol in his critical review of spontaneous cases of apparent precognition:

[It must] (1) have been told or recorded before fulfillment, or acted upon in such a manner as to afford evidence of foreknowledge; (2) include details so that chance fulfillment is rendered unlikely; (3) indicate fairly narrow limits of time for fulfillment, or else must contain such details as to fix the occasion of fulfillment, e.g. on visiting a certain place. And it must be of such a nature that (4) inference from considerably wider knowledge and with considerably enhanced powers of inference could not reasonably have been held to have afforded the foreknowledge; (5) suggestions, whether auto- or hetero-, conscious or unconscious, could not have brought about the fulfillment; (6) the information was not in the possession of any other person so that it could have been conveyed telepathically to the percipient, and the information in such cases would include the intention to perform certain actions; (7) it excludes hyperaesthesia of any extent which might reasonably be considered possible.[1]

Mr. Nicol noted that he, like Saltmarsh before him, had been unable to find a single case that met all those requirements. Proving prophecy is rather like proving the existence of purple cows. The whole idea is so incredible, that to convince anyone you must nail the hide to the barn door for all to see and test. And it only takes the hide of one purple cow to show that purple cows are possible. Catching the purple cow of prophecy seemed to be quite a formidable task. And it would be even more difficult to skin and nail it to the barn door. But I went to the British Museum Library in search of perfect prophecy. I found a German book published in 1849 that forecast a world war in 1938. That was not detailed enough to be evidential, but it was encouraging.

At this point, someone is liable to say, "How about Jeane Dixon's famous prophecy of President Kennedy's assassination?"

Mrs. Dixon's printed prophecy in *Parade* magazine of the assassination, the most famous prophecy of the twentieth century, is described in Ruth Montgomery's book *A Gift of Prophecy* (Morrow, 1966) on page 6: ". . . while two reporters from *Parade* magazine were interviewing her about predictions, she abruptly skipped over the intervening years and declared, 'A blue-eyed Democratic President elected in 1960 will be assassinated.'

"Startled by the bluntness of her words, the reporters suggested that they simply say he would 'die in office.'

" 'Say it as you like, but he will be assassinated,' she replied. Her prediction appeared in the *Parade* issue of March 11, 1956."

In my own research, my first requirement is that I see the printed prophecy with my own eyes; that way, I do not have to rely on anyone else's word. I checked with *Parade* magazine. The issue of March 11, 1956, contains not a single mention of Jeane Dixon whatsoever. Was it a hoax? Could it be that Mrs. Dixon did not remember correctly and Mrs. Montgomery had so little research background that it did not seem important to check it out? That also seemed incredible, but it proved to be true. The issue of May 13, 1956, is the one that contains Mrs. Dixon's prophecy, and it is different in precisely those details that had been formerly so convincing.

The prediction as actually printed reads: "As for the 1960 election, Mrs. Dixon thinks it will be dominated by labor and won by a Democrat. But he will be assassinated or die in office 'though not necessarily in his first term.' "

A key to Mrs. Dixon's prophecy had been thought of by many people over the years, including the parapsychologist Dr. Stanley Krippner when he was a twelve-year-old grade school student studying American presidents. He noticed a twenty-year presidential death cycle, in which presidents elected at twenty-year intervals from 1840 to the present had been assassinated or died in office, though not necessarily in the first term. As we shall see in Chapter 3, John Kennedy himself knew of the cycle before he was elected and had replied to a correspondent about it. As for his being a Democrat, Mrs. Dixon had a fifty-fifty chance of being right, for without the identifying detail of "blue eyes" he becomes merely a Democrat.

There is another difficulty in the way of evidentiality of prophecies of political assassinations, as noted by Dr. Ian Stevenson of the University of Virginia Parapsychology Division: "Political assassinations are not the best topic for assessing the accuracy of precognition. First, politically prominent persons are at high risk for assassination, and secondly, they are ordinarily much more thought about and dreamed about by many persons than are other strangers to the dreamers. There is thus a much greater likelihood of a chance correlation between a dream of a political figure and his murder or sudden death in another way." [2]

Thus, for prophecies of political assassinations, a great number of specific details must be included if it is to be nailed down. And in Saltmarsh's commentary on criteria of foreknowledge, he says: "Trivial details are evidentially more valuable than broad general features. Incorrect details do not necessarily detract much from evidential value." [3]

When I investigated other popular books on prophecy, I found the same kind of inaccuracy, deception, and even hoaxing. From the original editions at the British Museum Library I learned that Mother Shipton, a medieval prophetess famous for predicting events of the twentieth century, had actually never predicted anything beyond her own lifetime. A nineteenth-century editor had attributed prophecies to her, and these were altered again by writers in the 1960s—an intricate web of hoaxing for fun and profit. As columnist James Wechsler said, "The best stories are often ruined by that tedious process known as checking."

I turned to the Society for Psychical Research in London

and found there a wealth of unpublished material on prophecy. Although none of it was of sufficient quality to merit publication, it was fascinating. I learned that for nearly three-quarters of a century people had been registering prophecies at the SPR, sealing them in envelopes and waiting for Fulfillment Day when they would proudly announce to the SPR to open the envelope and see for themselves that the prediction was fulfilled. It seemed evident from the age of most of these predictions that the predictors had long since passed away, so I got permission from the SPR's Council to open them. My hopes of finding a prophet in print ebbed with each envelope that I opened. I did not find a single fulfilled prophecy that I could verify. Most of the predictions were for deaths of people whom nature had long since sent to the grave.

A grim note in the SPR Journal of June 1967 excited my interest, however. Dr. J. C. Barker of Shelton Hospital, Shrewsbury, had begun a collaboration with science editor Peter Fairley of the London *Evening Standard* to collect premonitions for a "Disaster Early Warning System." As a start they were appealing for further premonitions of the Aberfan disaster that had occurred in Wales when a coal tip slid down over the town of Aberfan and killed 144 people. Dr. Barker had collected a number of premonitions about this disaster, and although none of them alone was of evidential quality, the larger patterns suggested to him that if such premonitions were collected beforehand, then perhaps a warning could eventually be made to prevent such disasters.

I had conceived of the same plan some time before and wrote Dr. Barker with an offer of my cooperation with his project: "My plan will include the collection and analysis of as many predictions from as many psychics as possible to determine their emerging patterns, and eventually, I hope to arrive at broadly based predictions of general events—what I should term *prophecy*."

Dr. Barker replied that he was working on a book about the Aberfan predictions and shared with me his ideas for analyzing patterns of apparent precognition and collecting premonitions on a much larger scale, a project he felt would require a large staff and "computer time and money; but we have no money."

Nor did I, but I replied on November 8, 1967: "When I get back to the States in about a year, I hope to set up some sort of apparatus for collecting premonitions on quite a large scale. . . . For certainly, it seems to me that only a world-wide search for precognitive sensitives could turn up enough material for the injudicious maw of the computer."

My initial idea, as told to the parapsychological writer Martin Ebon on May 3, 1967, was this:

> Although our present knowledge of prophecy and pre-cognition is insufficient to explain it fully, it is still possible to make use of it—practical prophecy. Perhaps persons with prophetic talents could be trained, even as mediums have been trained, and indeed it is very possible that some mediums would be excellent subjects; if their prophetic utterances could be encouraged and developed; each according to his own lines of interest and talents, the results being constantly checked—perhaps then by cross checking independent prophecies a somewhat dependable pattern of prophecy would emerge. Further quantification could be achieved if a sufficient number of "oracular" subjects could build up a sufficiently large body of prophecies which would then be analyzed by a computer for the subtle intricate patterns that comprise our complex world.

That rather grand (grandiose?) idea was whittled down to size as I grappled with the realities of psychic experience. My initial frustration with being unable to find printed prophecies doubled as I tried to elicit prophecies from English mediums and fortune-tellers. I wanted prophecies about world events, but all they would tell me were predictions about my own life (more of this in Chapter 5). One unexpected bonus from this research was that Douglas Johnson, one of the best mediums at the College of Psychic Studies, invited me to attend his classes in psychic development where I learned to control and deepen my own psychic abilities.

Rather like a child with a new toy, I experimented continually with trying to make predictions for people and even prophecies of the sort that I had come to find. If none of the mediums would make prophecies, then perhaps I could do it myself. I began writing in predictions to Dr. Barker's Premonitions Bureau, keeping careful track of the details that led to the prediction. Just how did prophecy come into being? What were the psychological processes at work? How did it fit into the other patterns of behavior? These and other questions began to shift the focus of my investigation to relate prophecy to the inner workings of the mind.

My first lesson was that dramatic boners were easy to come by. One day when my landlady was talking about the London of years before when smog was a deadly menace, I had a sudden flash of memory of standing in a park in New York City on Thanksgiving Day in 1966 when eye-stinging smog covered the northeast. "It's going to happen again!" was my immediate response. I wrote Dr. Barker to expect a killer smog on Thanksgiving Day in 1967, a couple of months away.

Thanksgiving Day dawned (most fortunately) bright and clear. But at 1:00 in the afternoon I found myself in Belgrave Square going to an appointment. As I walked through the park-like square, I was suddenly enveloped in thick clouds of eye-smarting smoke from a pile of burning leaves. An interesting coincidence, at least, but the smoke was certainly not smog.

I became bolder in my prophecies. While reading an article in the London *Times* on October 22 about a new express train running from Osaka to Tokyo in Japan, I suddenly felt an alarming thought of *earthquake*. I visualized the train being derailed. The date of November 23 popped into my head. Again, I wrote Dr. Barker of this premonition. That afternoon I went to the Society for Psychical Research to do some research, and there in the library on top of a pile of periodicals was a magazine with a photo of the Osaka-Tokyo train. Sensing that this strange coincidence was meaningful, I went to the secretary's office to register my premonition with the SPR. It was about time, I thought, that the SPR should have at least one prediction on file before the event. They were skeptical but polite and filed away my premonition. November came and went. Months later, in March, there *was* a train derailed in Japan by an earthquake, but not the train I had specified. Probably a coincidence, I concluded; certainly not strong evidence for prophecy.

I was in for more frustration when I went to Germany in the spring of 1968 to study with Prof. Hans Bender at the Freiburg University Institute for Border Areas of Psychology. In Professor Bender's laboratory was a fraud-proof machine for testing precognition. Electronically operated, the machine would randomly flash one of five lights after a person had pressed a corresponding button in an attempt to predict which light would come on next. The results were automatically recorded. One young man at the Institute had been working with this machine for more than a year and had achieved a remarkably high score against chance. When I tried it over a period of several weeks, I got only chance scores. Never above, never below—just chance. But one morning, after weeks of frustration, I got revenge. The machine started to malfunction such that the randomly chosen light came on *before* the guess button was pushed. When I pushed the guess button that corresponded, the machine automatically racked up a "hit." With sweet revenge, I sat there and punched the buttons for a hundred straight hits. I then called the young man to come in to see how I had improved. His eyes bulged in disbelief—and I confessed I had managed to "cheat" the machine. Only that once did the machine ever malfunction in that way. Coincidence? Mind over matter? Whichever, I concluded that machine testing of precognition seemed to have little relation to whatever prophetic ability I might have.

I hasten to add that this is not necessarily so for others. One young British psychic, Malcolm Bessent, was able to get scores on an electronically operated precognition testing machine on the order of several thousand to one against chance —thereby "proving" that precognition is possible. But as the experimenter, Charles Honorton, noted,[4] it tells us nothing about the process of precognition nor the psychological workings of *psi* (psychic phenomena).

This experimental work, done at the Maimonides Medical Center in Brooklyn, was part of an intensive investigation of Bessent's psychic ability that began in the summer of 1969.[5] I first met Bessent in 1967 when he too was studying with Douglas Johnson in London, and we were both learning to give "psychic readings." One of his first readings was for me, and I was surprised to hear him say that he thought that one day we would be working together. I returned the favor of a psychic reading on July 8, 1968, and sent him a transcript of the recorded prediction: "You are going to New York for three months—spring basically. I think of Montague Ullman, head of the Maimonides Dream Lab. There are a couple of other characters poking around too. Some psychologists on the scene. Yes, I think you'll be involved with a program of testing."

As it turned out, we were both right, or nearly right. A Philadelphia inventor and a Canadian industrialist learned of Bessent's psychic ability two months after I gave him the reading, and then offered to finance him to come to New York to do experimental testing at the Maimonides Dream Laboratory. Bessent arrived in New York in June 1969.

Bessent's only comment at the time I made the prediction was, "What's the Maimonides Dream Lab?" I had met the directors of the lab, Dr. Ullman and Dr. Krippner, at the LSD-ESP conference the year before, so I knew a little about their work in dream telepathy. As it turned out, I too was to be an experimental subject for them, though I had no notion of that in July 1968.

When Bessent arrived in the States, we did a number of seminars in psychic development together—thus fulfilling his prediction for me.

Although our doing seminars together was certainly a self-fulfillment of Bessent's prediction, the fulfillment seemed out of his hands since it was initiated by the ideas (and money) of people he had not yet met at the time of the prediction. I first learned of this plan in December 1968 when I was in New York doing some experiments at the Maimonides Dream Laboratory. The director, Dr. Krippner, asked me, "Have you ever heard of an Englishman named Malcolm Bessent? He's scheduled to come here in May."

"Yes," I replied, "I not only know him but I even predicted he would come here then."

All this seemed oddly intermeshed in a series of coincidences that made me feel that chance was being strained to its limits.

2

The Clockwork Kerass

A *Kerass*, as devotees of Kurt Vonnegut's novels know, is a group of people who are unknowingly working together toward some common goal fostered by a larger cosmic influence. In Vonnegut's satire *Cat's Cradle* (and in the television drama "Between Time and Timbuktu") the concept of the Kerass is developed as a satirical religious belief. The way one learns that he is part of a Kerass is that meaningful coincidences happen between him and other members of the same Kerass. There is also the danger that one might mistake a chance coincidence for a meaningful coincidence, and in that case, one is involved in a *Granfaloon*, or false Kerass. Telling the Kerass from the Granfaloon would seem to be a high art.

If the term *Kerass* seems unlikely (actually it is the name of Vonnegut's next door neighbor), then one might prefer Carl Jung's term *synchronicity*, or perhaps the zoologist Paul Kammerer's term *seriality*. As Arthur Koestler writes in his book *The Roots of Coincidence* (Random House, 1972): "Both Kammerer and Jung postulate an a-causal principle which they consider of equal importance with causality in the destiny of man and of the world at large. The paradoxes of quantum physics may suggest that this postulate is no more preposterous than the theorems of modern science."

19

Nor, I might add, than the satirical theorem of Kurt Vonnegut.

I once wrote Kurt Vonnegut to ask where he got the idea of people being linked by meaningful coincidences. Was there any connection with ESP I wondered. His reply was startling.

> I have had one very flashy experience with telepathy or whatever, and my wife got the signals, too. They were evidently from my brother-in-law, who was being killed in a railroad train which had gone off an open drawbridge in New Jersey at the time. He died about 10:30 in the morning on a work day. . . . I suddenly left my study that morning, went the length of the house to the phone in the kitchen, put in a long distance call [from Massachusetts] to my brother-in-law. I had never telephoned him before, had no reason to call then. I telephoned him at his office, which he would never reach. There was a news flash over the radio about the railroad accident, without any details. I *knew* my brother-in-law had been on the train, though he had never taken the train before. I was on a plane within an hour, and had taken charge of his home and four children before the sun went down. My sister was a terminal cancer patient in a hospital at the time. She died the next day. My wife and I have since adopted and raised their children.

Vonnegut added that about two weeks before the incident, his wife kept coming up with the odd notion: "The refugees are coming, the refugees are coming." They came.

If it is horrific tragedies of life that spark ESP into operation, few could compare with Vonnegut's experience during World War II of being a prisoner of war in an underground slaughterhouse in Dresden when it was fire bombed. To ease the pain of witnessing such a holocaust, Vonnegut wrote the satirical novel *Slaughterhouse Five*, later made into a film. Interwoven as a minor theme in the life of Billy Pilgrim, the hero, is a philosophic conception that surpasses the science-fiction elements of previous Vonnegut novels on which it is based. Billy Pilgrim keeps getting "unstuck in time"—past, present, and future alternately are visited on Billy as the helpless "time-tripper." An event of the present triggers memories of similar events in the past—or it can trigger a "memory" of similar events in the future. In the film, when Billy sees a ski-masked person watching the takeoff of his plane, he has a sudden association with a future event—the crashing of the plane and his being found by a ski-masked rescuer in the snow. Billy's warning to the others that the plane will soon crash is, of course, laughed at. To me, however, this seems remarkably close to my own observations on the workings of prophecy (including the disregarding of a warning).

In yet another Vonnegut novel, *The Sirens of Titan*, the entire accomplishments of the human race—its monuments and great architectural works—are presented as being organized by a stranded spacecraft pilot of some supercivilization, the members of which live thousands of years. Actually, you see, all the great changes made by man on the face of the earth are but a code to signal this distant civilization to send a certain spare part to the stranded pilot. If I would dare to translate this concept into parapsychological (or even religious) terms, I might say that all human activity is guided toward certain goals by some intelligence so vastly greater than our own that we cannot begin to comprehend it. The existence of this plan or "blueprint" of humanity is what makes "time-tripping" possible. We tap (possibly through another dimension) future possibilities that preexist on a transcendental level. The coincidences or synchronicities that link our lives are manifestations of a universe so highly organized that literally *nothing* happens by chance. Like some incomprehensibly complex clockwork, the universe unfolds in time and space its inner plan that does not allow for accidents. "Chance" is but an illusion fostered by our incomplete knowledge of the universe's greater plan.

That is what I *might* say in attempting to appreciate Vonnegut's satire. I even begin to suspect that Vonnegut may be one of the most brilliant philosophers of our time. But let's look at some other thought about synchronicity.

In parapsychological circles Jung's theory of synchronicity is well known, if not generally accepted. The psychologist Dr. Gardner Murphy once voiced a sentiment that might be echoed among many other parapsychologists: How can you possibly explain something by calling it *acausal*—without cause? Doesn't that lead us back into primitive ways of supernatural thinking?

However, when I read the examples of meaningful coincidences in Jung's writings, it seems that what he means is that *synchronicity* is a meaningful coincidence without a normal (i.e., physical) cause. I would say, then, that synchronicity is the result of paranormal causes. More specifically, Jung postulates that such coincidences tend to emerge during emotionally charged events, which he terms *archetypal*. Certainly the synchronicities in Jung's own life tended to cluster around such emotion-laden events.

Jung gave an example of synchronicity in a 1945 letter to J. B. Rhine in which he answered Rhine's questions about his views on ESP:

> Viewed from the psychological standpoint, extra-sensory perception appears as a manifestation of the *collective unconscious*. This particular psyche behaves as if it were *one* and not as if it were split up into many individuals. It is *non-personal*. (I call it the "objective psyche.") It is the same everywhere and at all times. (If it were not so, comparative psychology would be impossible.) As it is not limited to the person, it is also not limited to the body. It manifests itself

therefore not only in human beings but also at the same time in animals and even in physical circumstances. (Cf. the oracle technique of the *I Ching* and character horoscopes.) I call these latter phenomena the synchronicity of archetypal events. For instance, I walk with a woman patient in a wood. She tells me about the first dream in her life that had made an everlasting impression upon her. She had seen a spectral fox coming down the stairs in her parental home. At this moment a real fox comes out of the trees not 40 yards away and walks quietly on the path ahead of us for several minutes. The animal behaves as if it were a partner in the human situation. (One fact is no fact, but when you have seen many, you begin to sit up.) [1]

There were also a number of synchronicities recorded by Jung that didn't seem to "mean" much at all (perhaps Vonnegut would identify them as signs of a Granfaloon). For instance, Jung once noticed that the number of his streetcar ticket was the same as that of a ticket to a concert that evening and that the same number came up in a telephone conversation; and this he gives as an example of synchronistic seriality, or series of events. But why is it meaningful?

I read that anecdote the morning of April 19, 1968, in Freiburg, Germany. My diary entry reads: "Having read an account of Jung's finding a synchronistic relationship between his streetcar ticket number, his theater ticket number, and a phone number, I studied my streetcar ticket number. It was 096960. Then I realized I was looking at it upside down. But it was the same: 096960. The number of the streetcar could also be read upside down: 111. But instead of finding a third number, like Jung, I nearly tripped over an ashcan with the name JUNG written on it."

It seemed as if Jung's theory were mocking me. But I wrote to a friend in the United States to send me a copy of Jung's *Interpretation of Nature and the Psyche*, which contains his essay on synchronicity. A month later, on May 19,

I had a brief image on going to sleep: "I receive the awaited book by Jung in a jiffy bag with a label on it showing a symbolic fish. I wondered if that were a connection with the Bollingen Foundation." (The Bollingen Foundation was the original U.S. publisher of the volume.)

Two days later, May 21, I was at the Freiburg Institute for Border Areas of Psychology to do some research. In the library I chanced to pick up an English-language paperback on personality assessment and noticed a chapter by Jung that was first published by the Bollingen Foundation. Going out onto the terrace, I laid the book down with that page open on a table. Then I noted that there was a fresh tablecloth decorated with symbolic fish. Instead of a Jung book and a *label* showing fish, there was a Jung book on a *table* showing fish. Marveling at the apparent synchronicity, I returned to my apartment and found to my surprise that my landlady had fashioned some symbolic fish out of paper and had hung them as a mobile from the ceiling lamp. When finally I received the book over a year later in the States (it came in a jiffy bag), I was delighted to learn that Jung was first inspired to his theory of synchronicity by a series of incidents involving the symbol of the fish. I was hooked. For me, at least, the "meaning" of this synchronicity was: Pay attention to coincidences.

Prof. Hans Bender, director of the Freiburg Institute, had long been paying attention to coincidences. He had conversed with Jung about synchronicity and paranormal phenomena a few months before Jung's death in December 1960. Professor Bender had noticed synchronistic events in his own life, and in our conversations about prophecy and ESP we made frequent references to the synchronicity theory. Professor Bender stressed the relationship of synchronistic events to what he termed *organizing archetypes*—countless motifs of life that have been repeated through the generations of man.

Tracing the origin of his ideas about the archetype to Plato, Jung added the concept that "archetypes are not disseminated only by tradition, language, and migration, but . . . they can rearise spontaneously, at any time, at any place, and without any outside influence. . . .

"There are present in every psyche forms which are unconscious but nonetheless active—living dispositions, ideas in the Platonic sense, that preform and continually influence our thoughts and feelings and actions." [2]

Jungian psychology generally uses the word *archetype* to define a few predominate concepts, such as the *animus* for the male aspect of a woman, or *anima* for the female aspect of a man. Yet, when pressed on just what *is* an archetype, Jung explained to an interviewer that the range of archetypes was vast. He gave the admittedly rare example of a king being killed while fording a stream as a recurrent theme of life. Jung also identified Freudian concepts of sexuality as archetypes but maintained that there were many more in addition.

I use the word *archetype* in its basic meaning of preformed ideas that tend to recur. There are human archetypal situations: birth, death, marriage, divorce. There are archetypal roles of life: soldier, statesman, poet, philosopher, hero, slave. Drama of classical times relied almost wholly on such archetypal roles, parts that today critics would call stereotypes.

Our patterns of life can be broken down into such individual archetypal roles, just as our genetic heritage can be analyzed for its sources. A nose from father, a mouth from mother, a temper like grandfather, and so on. Collectively, then, the various roles that a human being plays through his lifetime could be called his pattern of life. And if those roles preexist as archetypes, then this preexistent set of roles together form a "blueprint" of life. In addition, each of us has his own individual archetypes—patterns of experience that tend to recur. On the commonest level these might be termed habits. Some people are late for work every morning. At another level, one might speak of neuroses. Jack quits his job every two years because he is afraid of advancement. But there are healthy varieties of recurring experience as well, compulsions of a positive type. Bill runs for councilman every two years (until he finally makes it).

The longer an archetype has been established in human life, the greater its force. The most established of these (i.e., primitive) we term *instincts*.

In the development of his hypothesis of the Oedipus complex—that a male child unconsciously wanted to put his father out of the way so that he could attain his mother in love—Freud borrowed the archetypal role from Sophocles' play. In the play itself, however, a strong emphasis was placed on man's inability to escape his predestined fate. The oracle prophesied that the child would murder his father and marry his mother. And it was by "coincidence" that Oedipus met his father at a narrow pass and, after an argument, slew him. The Greeks completely accepted the concept that each man has a "blueprint" of life that controls his destiny and that is capable of being precognized. The fulfillment of the prophecies generally involved "chance" coincidences.

Just as so-called instincts compel a person into actions of life, so do archetypal roles. A fictional description of how this works was given by the modern Greek writer Nikos Kantzantzakis in his novel *The Greek Passion*. When townspeople of a Greek village decided to put on a passion play of the death of Christ, each person was assigned a role to play. As they began rehearsals, the players strangely found that they were beginning to play the Passion's roles in real life. The culminating scene was the death of the actor playing Christ at the hands of the others.

Another modern Greek provides a more familiar real-life example: Aristotle Onassis seems to be playing the role of

Jason. Like Jason, a commander of a ship, Onassis has gone to a foreign land to bring back the queen, Jacqueline Kennedy, playing the role of Medea. Like Medea, Jacqueline Onassis has been witness to the slaying of one she loved. The demonic aspects of Medea are scaled down. Unlike Medea, who slew the sons of Jason, Mrs. Onassis does not kill the son of Onassis; but the boy does die in an airplane crash. Medea was jealous of Jason's marriage to a princess. Mrs. Onassis might have found herself in a similar situation with Onassis's friendship with Maria Callas, whose most dramatic filmed role has been that of Medea. If the archetypal roles they play continue to hold their effect, then one might expect that Onassis will die in some accident involving a ship (or airplane) he owns, as did Jason die when his beached ship fell over on him. Then, like Medea, Mrs. Onassis would fly to her homeland.

The way we reenact archetypal roles need not be so precise. As Freud pointed out, men often play the role of Oedipus in the so-called Oedipus complex; or women play the role of Electra. Eugene O'Neill's play *Mourning Becomes Electra* again shows the fulfillment of archetypal roles. The inspiration for this play had come from the real-life drama of O'Neill's own family.

Long before I knew anything about Jung's theory of synchronicity, I had become aware of periods in my life when astonishing coincidences stunned me into wondering if they had any significance. I first became aware of this in the spring of 1965 when I flew from New York to San Francisco for a few weeks. Within a short time I managed to accidentally meet at least a dozen friends who I had no idea were in California. When I went to a cabaret, I was seated by the hostess next to a sailor with whom I began talking. He had been my paperboy in Akron, Ohio, many years before and asked after my parents. He was in San Francisco for only one day.

Crossing a street, I chanced to look beside me, and there was a friend from the army I had last seen in Germany. Several others turned up. Looking at a movie poster in Berkeley at the University of California, I heard a voice from behind: "I still have that book you loaned me in Frankfurt." I ran into another army friend in a book store, and two others in a restaurant. I very nearly bowled over a young man in the street as I was emerging from a telephone booth; he was a friend from New York. At a parade I was sighted by a couple from the University of Akron, and they invited me to stay for a while in their home. And, to steal a Vonnegut phrase, so it goes.

Later I heard similar tales from others. Perhaps my favorite is told by Martin Ebon, the parapsychologist. When on a visit to India, he had a letter of introduction to a government official, but unfortunately the official could not be reached. Later the car Ebon was riding in ran out of gas, and his chauffeur flagged down the first car to pass. It was the car of the sought-after official.

A beguiling aspect of synchronicity is the way it happens when its existence has to be demonstrated. Some months ago I was talking in a crowded room with a stranger about the theory of synchronicity. I gave him a number of examples, but he remained unconvinced. After all, synchronicity seems most illogical. "I can think of an alternate hypothesis that is better," he replied and began to speak of Levi-Bruhl, the French writer. Precisely at the moment that he uttered that phrase, or perhaps a fraction of a second before, another man nearby said exactly the same words in the context of a conversation he was carrying on with someone else. A brief moment of anger was experienced by the second man when he questioned the man I was speaking with: "Are you mocking me? What's wrong with my idea?" It took a few minutes of explanation on our part before the second man was convinced that it was merely "coincidence" that his words were exactly echoed in another conversation.

"See," I smiled at my puzzled adversary," that's what I mean by synchronicity."

"Maybe there is something to it after all," he reluctantly replied.

In May 1971 I gave a talk to the Spiritual Frontiers Fellowship national convention in Chicago on prophecy and synchronicity. The speaker who was to follow me was Marcus Bach, whose recent book on serendipity had been sold to me that morning by an enterprising fan of his. Seizing the synchronistic opportunity, I explained that *serendipity*—the art of finding something valuable when looking for something else—is but a special form of synchronicity. That afternoon, waiting for a plane back to New York, I read the book. Getting up to leave the airport lounge, I chanced to glance over the shoulder of a woman who was reading a national newspaper. She was reading an article about me. Unable to resist the temptation, I reached over her shoulder and pointed out an inaccuracy in the article. She turned around and gave me a very startled look indeed. "Oh, you look just like your picture. Isn't it a coincidence that you should happen along just as I was reading this."

"Yes," I replied, "that's an example of synchronicity, as in this book I'm reading. In fact I was just lecturing about it this morning."

She was still shaking her head as I walked away.

On the morning of August 22, 1972, I was starting work on this chapter and thinking of how best to illustrate a synchronistic episode. The problem still unresolved, I went to a luncheon appointment I had made a week before with Robert Nelson, director of the Central Premonitions Registry (see Chapter 4). I had a number of questions I wanted to ask him about the recent parapsychological meetings in Moscow, which he had attended. On the way, I chanced to glance at a stack of *Wall Street Journals* and saw an article on the Central Premonitions Registry, which included some precognitions I had sent them. When we met, Mr. Nelson had a copy also. We went to a popular midtown restaurant and began our conversation about parapsychology in the Soviet Union. Unnervingly, two gentlemen seated next to us were also carrying on a conversation about parapsychology in the Soviet Union. Mr. Nelson described to me a demonstration of psychokinesis (moving an object by will) that he witnessed in Moscow. The two strangers were talking about psychokinetic demonstrations in Russia. Mr. Nelson and I shifted our conversation to precognition and theories of time; the other two were now talking about theories of time.

Unable to bear it any longer, we introduced ourselves and inquired about their interests in parapsychology. They told us about their new organization that was designed to help people develop their psychic abilities and mentioned a young researcher who was doing so-called Kirlian photography—a topic thoroughly discussed at the Moscow meetings. And so it was by "chance" that we learned of some very interesting parapsychological work. It was also fortuitous that we were able to show them the *Wall Street Journal* article about our own work.

Nearly everyone I have asked has some such interesting coincidence to relate. Is it merely chance? Or should we ask, "Is chance merely the outcome of random events or is there some subtle pattern of events that might lend itself to prediction of events?"

It seems to me that synchronicity cannot be easily divorced from ESP—the two are often intermixed in such a way that it is not feasible to distinguish them. For instance, in May 1972 I went to Dayton, Ohio, with Herbert Greenhouse to help publicize his book *Premonitions: A Leap into the Future* (Geis, 1972) on the nationwide television program "The Phil Donahue Show." Before the show, Mr. Donahue stated forthrightly that he was a disbeliever in ESP. He asked me what predictions I had for the future. I mentioned only one: I expected very soon now the resignation of J. Edgar Hoover from the FBI. During the live telecast, a news bulletin was flashed on the screen, announcing that J. Edgar Hoover had just died. Off camera, Mr. Donahue looked quizzically at me. "Well," I said, "Hoover resigned the only way he could." We didn't mention my prediction during the rest of the show, but Mr. Donahue's antagonism toward psychic phenomena palpably evaporated.

Lovers meeting for the first time is certainly an archetypal situation par excellence. And when it happened to me, I noticed a lot of synchronicities. In August 1966, when I was living in Greenwich Village in New York, I noticed that chairs were being set up for a concert in Washington Square Park. Deciding to stay to listen, I managed to secure the end of a park bench next to an elderly Polish gentleman, with whom I struck up a conversation. He was also talking to a young woman on the other side, and finally, through him, the young woman and I were introduced. Later we went for coffee along with her girlfriend. We discovered that we both worked for companies named ABC: mine was American Book Company; Iris's was American Broadcasting Company. We had both attended a lecture on prophecy by Jeane Dixon a few weeks before. A co-worker of mine who suddenly and mysteriously had left the company turned out to be working with her girlfriend. Later I discovered that the Polish gentleman had been telling her how his daughter had met her husband at a concert in the park.

Now, some weeks before this I had noticed an advertisement for what was then a daring and "fun" idea: a computer dating service. I had sent in my name and filled out a questionnaire but had discarded the names sent me since by now I was dating Iris. But then shortly after Iris had moved to a new address, I received one more card with a girl's name and address: she lived in the same building and directly above Iris.

After Iris and I were married in April 1967, I was rummaging through some old papers and discovered some predictions I had written down in November 1965, mostly about world events. But one was circled as having nothing to do with the questions I had asked myself: "You will marry in 1967."

I cannot make too much of that, of course, since it is perfectly conceivable that I fulfilled my own prophecy, albeit unconsciously. But yet, I began to think, if an archetypal situation preexisted in some transcendental dimension, then perhaps that would account for its being able to be predicted. The synchronicities, on the other hand, would arise—according to Jung's observations—during the time the archetype was being fulfilled in reality.

How would one go about experimenting to find out if this were true or not? Jung tried an experiment in astrology that gave interesting results. In astrological lore, certain signs are more compatible or less compatible for personal relationships. To test this, Jung compared the birth data of a group of married couples with those of a group of non-married couples. Initially, with a fairly small sample, the astrological predictions seemed to hold up. But when the sample was greatly enlarged, then the relationships dropped down to a chance level. Not daunted by this, Jung said that it reminded him of the type of results that J. B. Rhine was getting with his ESP card-guessing experiments: initial high scoring with a drop as the experiments continued (the decline effect). Jung suggested that his initial excitement in this experiment (the archetypal situation) was productive of the high correlation. Jung's implication, that ESP card-guessing measures only the emotional excitement of a new and interesting experiment, has never been taken seriously by parapsychologists. If they *did* take it seriously, then they would have to say that what they were measuring was not extrasensory perception but some more fundamental quality of the psyche's interaction with its environment.

As a matter of fact, one prominent British parapsychologist, the biologist Sir Alister Hardy, does suggest that card-guessing tests may be measuring something akin to *luck*. He adds that such quantitative testing may have provided "a wonderful mine of material for the study of a very remarkable new principle." [3]

I have talked with a number of parapsychologists about such a possibility, if synchronicity can be linked to Sir Alister's "remarkable new principle," and have generally been reproved for such heretical thinking. The theoretical models already in use in parapsychology for ESP and psychokinesis (PK) assume an awesome intricacy, especially when they are combined to explain the success of divination systems like the *I Ching*. However, one should keep in mind that ESP and PK are themselves mysteries when it comes to having any generally acceptable model of explanation. Therefore explaining synchronicity (or even luck) by ESP and PK is tantamount to explaining the unknown by the unknown.

What is important, however, is that an increasing number of researchers are beginning to pay attention to this fundamental quality of man's interaction with his environment. Dr. Rex Stanford of the University of Virginia Parapsychology Division has coined the term *psi-mediated instrumental response* (PMIR) for the type of phenomena I am calling synchronistic. Dr. Stanford, for instance, gives this example of unconscious use of psi:

Police called in a supposed witness to testify in an armed-robbery case. When he arrived in court he realized he knew nothing about the case being tried, but he *did* know something about the defendant: that he was the man who had robbed him of $1,000 about two months earlier but who had never been apprehended in connection with that crime. The man called as the witness promptly charged the defendant with this additional crime. The "witness's" name had been given by the police to the prosecuting attorney (as connected with the original case) purely by mistake—a mistake which resulted in the apparent solution of an unsolved crime." [4]

Ultimately the success of any theoretical construction depends on whether it can predict the future outcome of events consistently.

A phenomenon of comparable difficulty to investigate in the laboratory might be *love*. Nearly everybody admits to some experience of love, yet it has never been demonstrated scientifically in the laboratory. There are no equations that can tell us if a boy and girl, on first meeting, will (a) fall in love; (b) take an instant dislike to each other; or (c) remain indifferent to each other. Yet in some cultures matchmakers have at least a modicum of success in introducing young people who then marry. But this is an intuitive art, not a science. Love obdurately remains as much of a mystery as ESP, locked in the unconscious, yet occasionally revealing tantalizing clues to its very real existence.

If love is the most forceful archetype in life, the most forceful archetype of all is the end of life—death, especially violent death. Some very strange things happen at death. Jung termed these events synchronistic. Parapsychologists term them *crisis telepathy, premonitions, psychokinesis* (as, say, when a clock stops), *crisis apparitions*, and also *death bed visions*. By far the greatest proportion of spontaneous ESP cases collected in the last ninety years pertain to death and the threat of death.

Harvesting the greatest number of these related occurrences are assassinations of political leaders.

In ancient times the assassination archetype par excellence was the stabbing of Caesar in 44 A.D. The historian Plutarch gives a full account of the strange occurrences that accompanied the assassination, many of them familiar to us through Shakespeare's play: the soothsayer's prediction to Caesar, "Beware the Ides of March"; the premonitory dream of Caesar's wife; and the appearance of a brilliant comet in the sky.

Although one may easily discount some of the phenomena as products of a superstitious age, which required suitable signs from the heavens to announce the death of a prince, yet there may be grains of truth imbedded in Plutarch's description:

> For many strange prodigies and apparitions are said to have been observed shortly before this event. As to the lights in the heavens, the noises heard in the night, and the wild birds which perched in the forum, these are not perhaps worth taking notice of in so great a case as this. Strabo, the philosopher, tells us that a number of men were seen, looking as if they were heated with fire, contending with each other; that a quantity of flame issued from the hand of a soldier's servant, so that they who saw it thought he must be burnt, but that after all he had no hurt. As Caesar was sacrificing, the victim's heart was missing, a very bad omen, because no living creature can subsist without a heart. . . . The day before his assasination . . . there arose a question what sort of death was the best. At which he immediately, before any one could speak, said, "A sudden one."

Perhaps one of the most interesting aspects of Plutarch's description of "prodigies" and coincidences is that he evidently felt that there *should* be strange events constellated about the death of Caesar; one almost gets the feeling that if there had not been any, he would have invented some to assuage his readers' beliefs in omens and signs from the heavens.

The ancients interpreted such remarkable coincidences as the work of divinities—miracles of the gods. Carl Jung would have explained them as acausal synchronicity—miracles of chance. My own interpretation combines those views: What we call *chance coincidence* is the result of—and evidence of—a divinity that organizes all creation through the operation of archetypes.

Where Kurt Vonnegut sees as satire the organizing of human life by some supremely indifferent outer-spaceman, I see the Clockwork Kerass as the product of an infinite intelligence endowed with a sense of humor and of tragedy.

Eileen Garrett once asked me if I thought life were authored by a tragedian. "No," I replied, "it's written by a tragicomedian." As in the ancient Greek theater, tragedies alternate with comedies. The roles we play—the archetypes of life—may make us cry or laugh.

It depends on which roles we try out for.

3

Archetypes of Assassination [1]

The archetypes of assassination spring from the dawn of time. The violent death of Caesar provides the basic pattern of assassination in Western culture, a culmination to the archetypal role of the hero who must die.

Echoing the assassination of Caesar was the fate of President Abraham Lincoln in 1865. His assassin, John Wilkes Booth, had often played an assassin of Caesar on the stage. And synchronistically, as if to make up for Booth's crime, his brother Edwin once saved Lincoln's son Tad from being run over by a train. Lincoln's assassination began a new variation of the archetypal pattern that was to be repeated three times a century later—the assassinations of President Kennedy, Martin Luther King, and Robert Kennedy.

The archetypal role of the hero who must die seems to go through many variations, each one drawing upon a past fulfillment of the archetype and adding something new, thus becoming a modified model. If the archetypal model can be precisely identified, then one may be able to predict further developments on a logical basis, such as the final fate of Sirhan Sirhan. The key to recognizing the precise archetypal model is in finding meaningful coincidences (or synchronicities) that link the present with the past situation. Evidence that Lincoln, J. F. Kennedy, Martin Luther King, and R. F. Kennedy were playing out preexistent archetypal roles as part of their "blue-prints" of life comes from the singular fact that their assassinations were all foretold. And in accordance with Jung's view that archetypal situations give rise to synchronicities, each of the assassinations was accompanied by strange coincidences.

The assassinations of Presidents Lincoln and Kennedy were part of a larger presidential death cycle that began with the election of William Henry Harrison in 1840.[2] One possible reason put forward for this was a curse put upon Harrison by a Shawnee Indian prophet after Harrison defeated the Shawnees at the battle of Tippecanoe in 1811. Harrison died of pneumonia in 1841, a month after his inauguration. Since that time—without exception—every president elected at a twenty-year interval has died in office. President Lincoln, elected 1860, was assassinated in 1865; President Garfield, elected in 1880, was assassinated in 1881; President McKinley, reelected in 1900, was assassinated in 1901; President Harding, elected in 1920, died in 1923; President Roosevelt, reelected in 1940, died in 1945; and President Kennedy, elected in 1960, was assassinated in 1963. A conservative estimate of the odds of this against chance is a hundred to one.

As a candidate, John Kennedy had been warned of that death cycle but had replied that if every candidate took such a warning seriously, there would be no one willing to serve as president. So it was with full knowledge of that strange death cycle that John Kennedy was elected in 1960—to follow the fate of the president elected in 1860, Abraham Lincoln.

President Kennedy has often been compared to President Lincoln as a champion of civil rights for Negroes, but far deeper and stranger patterns emerge to link them in these astonishing coincidences:

• Lincoln was elected to Congress in 1847, Kennedy in 1947.

- Both were over six feet tall and had been in military service.
- The names of Lincoln and Kennedy both contain seven letters.
- The wife of each president lost a son when she was first lady.
- Both presidents were shot in the head from behind on a Friday in the presence of their wives.
- Lincoln's secretary advised him not to go to the theater; Kennedy's secretary, whose name was Lincoln, advised him not to go to Dallas.
- Both Lincoln and Kennedy were succeeded by Southerners named Johnson, born a hundred years apart.

The synchronistic patterns extend also to the assassins, John Wilkes Booth and Lee Harvey Oswald:

- The names of John Wilkes Booth and Lee Harvey Oswald both contain fifteen letters.
- Booth was born in 1839, Oswald in 1939.
- Both Oswald and Booth were shot down while held by their captors.
- The killer of Booth, Boston Corbett, was later declared insane; the killer of Oswald, Jack Ruby, later pleaded insanity.
- Oswald and Booth were both Southerners.
- Booth was involved in a conspiracy; Oswald was suspected of being part of a conspiracy.

The paths of Lincoln and Kennedy were parallel even after death: painstaking research done at the order of Jacqueline Kennedy insured that every detail of Kennedy's funeral followed that of Lincoln's.

That was planned coincidence. The chance coincidences that made the assassinations possible seem a conspiracy of fate:

- By chance John Wilkes Booth had gone to Ford's Theater that morning to pick up his mail when he overheard that

Lincoln planned to attend that night, giving him the necessary time to make preparations for the murder. By chance, it seems, the soldier who was supposed to be guarding Lincoln's box left his post to have a drink at a nearby bar. By chance he had been in that same bar earlier—at the same time that Booth was there, drinking courage for his fatal act.

• The deadly accuracy of Oswald's rifle was made possible not by his marksmanship, but by a chance coincidence. The rifle found in the Dallas book depository had a defect in the telescopic lens that *was perfectly compensated for* by the curving path of President Kennedy's automobile. If Kennedy had not been wearing a back brace, he would have slumped down after the first, nonfatal bullet hit his back, passed through his neck and, according to the Warren Report, wounded Governor Connally. If Kennedy had not worn that brace, the first in line of fire for the fatal shot would have been his wife, Jacqueline.

The sorrowing figure of Jacqueline Kennedy became the emblem of that American tragedy. But the tragedies were to multiply, and she was to attend two more funerals.

The next victim was Martin Luther King. Like Presidents Lincoln and Kennedy, he was most remembered for his outstanding achievements in gaining civil rights for Negroes. As many of his followers feared, he met their fate as well: on April 4, 1968, a rifle shot ripped into his jaw and severed his spinal cord as he came out onto his motel room balcony in Memphis. Paralleling President Kennedy's assassination, the rifle left behind was quickly traced to its owner, Eric Starvo Galt, an alias of James Earl Ray.

Other aliases of Ray include *Harvey* Lowmyer and *John Will*ard, reminiscent of Lee *Harvey* Oswald and *John Wil*kes Booth. Ray's aliases were not fictitious. Several of them have been traced to men all closely resembling Ray, all living a few blocks from each other in Toronto.

During the flights of Oswald and Ray from the scene of the crime, the police created as much mystery as anyone. An early police radio report of Oswald's description is completely baffling since the police did not yet know his identity; they have never been able to trace the source of that description. An early police radio report of "Galt's" flight in a white Mustang is also baffling since police deny there ever was such a report—though an abandoned Mustang allegedly belonging to "Galt" was later found.

Of the synchronistic patterns linking Ray and Oswald, the rumors of conspiracy seem the strongest. Oswald's early death at the hands of Ruby generated so many charges of conspiracy that at last one came to trial—charges brought by James Garrison. Even now, charges of conspiracy in King's assassination still persist.

The most striking synchronistic feature of the assassinations—of Lincoln, J. F. Kennedy, King, R. F. Kennedy—is that each assassination was foretold. Apparently sensing their own tragic role in that archetypal pattern, Lincoln, John Kennedy, and Martin Luther King all made statements shortly before their death that were prophetic of it.

An action by Robert Kennedy, moreover, is suggestive of a premonition: when a German newsman mentioned to him that he had met John Kennedy during his Berlin visit, Robert burst into tears, an uncharacteristic action. A few hours later he suffered a fatal bullet wound in his head. As *Newsweek* noted: "The wounds were eerily close to John Kennedy's. The stigmata at last were made real."

In the case of Lincoln, it was the dream made real. A few days before his assassination he related to a friend a dream in which he came upon a funeral. "Who is dead in the White House?" he asked. "The President," was the answer; "he was killed by an assassin."

On the very day he was killed, Lincoln remarked to a

bodyguard: "Do you know, I believe there are men who want to take my life. And I have no doubt they will do it." On the day that John Kennedy was killed, he remarked: "If anybody wanted to shoot the President of the United States, it would not be a very difficult job—all one has to do is get on a high building some day with a telescopic sight and there's nothing anybody can do to defend such an attempt."

Other premonitions of President Kennedy's death could fill a book and probably one day will. The most famous premonition was that of Jeane Dixon, "the Washington seeress," whose story is recounted in Ruth Montgomery's *A Gift of Prophecy*. In October 1963 she told psychiatrist Dr. F. R. Riesenmann and Ruth Montgomery of a vision in which the vice-presidential plaque was removed from Lyndon Johnson's door. The man responsible for that had a two-syllable name with five or six letters: "The second letter was definitely an *s*, and the first looked like an *o*. . . . The last letter ended with a little curve that went straight up."

Another seer, British clairvoyant John Pendragon, wrote President Kennedy on October 25, 1963, quoting his prediction already published in the British *Fate Annual*: "The President may make powerful enemies among his own people, and I would not rule out the possibility of an attempted assassination or worse if he is caught off his guard. There may be a strange turning of the Wheel of Fate, for it is just a century since . . . President Lincoln was shot by a madman, Booth, in April, 1865."

Pendragon urged Kennedy to strengthen his bodyguard against assassination attempts, but received no answer.

There were countless other premonitions, many witnessed (although not documented), such as the following case.

A young New York office worker, Vito Gennaro, had voted for Nixon in the 1960 presidential election. When an office co-worker told him that John Kennedy had won,

Vito told me he found himself replying, as if with another's voice: "Oh my God, he's going to be shot in the head!"

In the presence of several witnesses, all known to me, the same man saw an image of Martin Luther King over the head of a Negro woman in the group. Again, Vito was horrified at what he heard his voice saying, something they had never discussed: "I fear that Martin Luther King is going to be assassinated sooner than we think!" That day was March 30, 1968.

On April 2 a reporter from the *Chattanooga News-Free Press* was in the office of Ralph "Doc" Anderson, a Rossville, Georgia, clairvoyant who had successfully predicted in 1944 the time of President Roosevelt's death and the date for the ending of World War II. On the television set in Anderson's office there flashed a picture of Martin Luther King. Anderson spoke out: "He will be dead by the middle of the month!"

On the morning of April 4 the wife of an eminent British philosopher, who was residing with her husband temporarily in the United States, told him of a strange dream the night before. In her dream she had been watching some "ghastly" television program—which she avers she never does—when the program was interrupted by the news that de Gaulle had been assassinated. Perhaps her subconscious had substituted the more familiar name of de Gaulle for King, for late that afternoon she was visited by her teen-aged daughter, who cajoled her into watching a "ghastly" TV program—which was interrupted by the tragic news of Dr. King's assassination.

The night before, Martin Luther King had spoken these prophetic words:

> We've got some difficult days ahead. But it really doesn't matter with me now. Because I've been to the mountaintop. I won't mind. Like anybody, I would like to live a long life. Longevity has its place. But I'm not concerned about that now. I just want to do God's will. And He's allowed me to

go to the mountain. And I've looked over, and I've seen the Promised Land. I may not get there with you, but I want you to know tonight that we as a people will get to the Promised Land. So I'm happy tonight. I'm not fearing any man. Mine eyes have seen the glory of the coming of the Lord!

Soon after the news of King's assassination reached me in Freiburg, Germany, I recorded a dream on April 6: "A group of people were in danger. They found a man who could ward off the dangerous rays by holding a large towel (aegis?) that fluttered and magically stopped the rays. But finally the people couldn't stand it—the man was ritually murdered by a girl who tore his heart out with a knife. Could there be a connection with the murder of Martin Luther King the day before? Will another be martyred?"

On April 11 I tried to interpret the dream: "This dream may presage the assassination of a third prominent American, one who has connections with JFK and Luther King—someone young, married, who espouses equal rights for Negroes. Could that other martyr be Bobby Kennedy? His assassination would link synchronistically. The initials of the three— KKK—would be symbolic of the divisive racialist fever in the U.S. Could the Kennedy brothers have a synchronistic link with the Gracchi of ancient Rome?" (The Gracchi brothers were two Roman statesmen of the second century B.C. who were killed in riots [one in 133 B.C., the other in 121 B.C.]; both had been advocates of social reform.)

The symbolic form of that dream might be traced to the archetype of the hero who must die, especially as it developed in ancient Greece. The aegis was a magic goatskin that could protect people from harm. The ritual act of cutting out the heart as a sacrifice might be identified with the ancient Aztec rite. A few days before the dream I had read a (spurious) story of a woman on LSD cutting out the heart of her baby, which probably gave rise to that aspect of the dream.

This dream came shortly after I had begun to record dreams on an experimental basis to see if any might prove precognitive and also to explore with Prof. Hans Bender at the Freiburg Institute for Border Areas of Psychology the possibility of synchronicity appearing in dreams. I felt that synchronicity and precognition might be closely linked and so was looking for some way to test this hypothesis. The opportunity came on April 20, when a number of seemingly synchronistic coincidences prompted me to write Professor Bender a memo that day:

> On April 20th, I picked up a *Bildzeitung* [German newspaper], whose headline was Gewalt muss sein! [Violence must be!] Then I bought the International Herald Tribune of April 19th, whose main story was the FBI's manhunt for the suspected murderer of Martin Luther King, Eric Starvo Galt [alias of James Earl Ray]. One of the murderer's aliases, *Harvey* Lowmyer, reminded me of JFK's assassin, Lee *Harvey* Oswald. His other alias, *John Will*ard, reminded me of Lincoln's assassin, *John Wil*kes Booth. The assassin's last name, Galt, reminded me of Gewalt in the *Bildzeitung*, and as I looked down the newspaper column at Galt's name, I noticed in the next column a mention of *Bildzeitung* [in] an article about two victims of violence.
>
> Scanning across the Herald's columns on that line I noticed the following words: "Dr. King, killed by a single bullet/Both were hit . . . ./Kennedy [R.F.]/believed dead. Two more Americans and/the former President . . ./from the North . . ./. . . ten-week . . !"
>
> If my noticing those words is a synchronicity and not a chance coincidence, then it is a prediction that Robert Kennedy will be shot. If the last words I noticed are part of the event, then the time should be in ten weeks.

Actually, the time turned out to be nine weeks from King's assassination.

I know of no way to assess the odds against chance of this

synchronistic episode, but a number of factors seemed to dovetail in a way that makes chance coincidence unlikely: (a) I was looking for a way to test the hypothesis that synchronicity and precognition are linked; (b) Only in Germany could I obtain the two necessary newspapers that cross-linked to draw my attention to reading across the columns of the *Tribune* on one particular line; (c) I had been reading Dr. Stanley Krippner's article on the twenty-year presidential death cycle and thinking about the possibility of its being extended further; (d) I had never before thought of reading a newspaper that way in search of any oracular message; (e) I was studying with perhaps the only professor in the world who had a deep interest in synchronicity.

Another factor was doubtless my frustration at being unable to find a fulfilled prophecy that was recorded before its fulfillment. Accordingly, on May 20, I wrote the London *Evening Standard's* Premonition Bureau with my premonition that Robert Kennedy would be the victim of an assassination attempt within two months.

On the morning of May 25 I rose at 5:00 A.M. to record some vividly remembered dreams. Two of them seemed to be related. In the first dream an American Indian fired a rifle through a grating to murder a person. In the second dream Robert Kennedy became me, walking through a hallway; dirt fell from an overhead grating, which I associated with a kitchen hallway in my boyhood home. I commented in my dream diary: "A single rifle shot from a grating might be connected with the dirt shifting down from the grating in the second dream. It may be precognitive, but in a very distorted form. The dirt coming down seems ominous." I took the American Indian to be symbolic that "the assailant will not be a member of a group commonly thought of as anti-Kennedy."

And as bizarre as it may sound, the American Indian may also be symbolic of the curse put on President Harrison—

which may have started the twenty-year death cycle—by a Shawnee Indian prophet.

There were also a number of literal correspondences between the dreams and Kennedy's assassination on June 5, 1968, in a kitchen hallway of the Ambassador Hotel in Los Angeles.

First Dream	*The Assassination*
1. "... it was dark ..."	1. It was after midnight.
2. "... the killer ... hid ..."	2. Sirhan hid beside an ice machine.
3. "... to fire one shot from a rifle to murder the person."	3. A shot fired into Kennedy's brain proved fatal.
4. "He thought of firing more shots."	4. He not only thought of firing more shots, but actually did.
5. "He was a person people did not suspect."	5. Sirhan was not suspected.

Second Dream	*The Assassination*
6. "... a party is planned."	6. A party was planned.
7. "Many people came, including Sen. Robert Kennedy ..."	7. Kennedy was accompanied by many people.
8. "... I go into a central hall connecting all the rooms ..."	8. Kennedy went into a central hall connecting the Ballroom, the kitchen, and the Colonial Room.
9. "... the first room ... where a small group of young people are."	9. In the first room, the Ballroom, were many young people.
10. "Kennedy must be in the other room, I think, and head for it."	10. Kennedy was heading for the other room.

11. Dirt was falling in the central hall.	11. The "dirty deed" was committed in the central hall.

Probably the greatest discrepancy between the dreams and the actual assassination is, in the first dream, a rifle firing a fatal shot through a grating. I had assumed that this was a dream distortion until recently when I read of the coroner's testimony at Sirhan Sirhan's trial. The coroner who examined Kennedy's body testified that the fatal bullet was fired *one to three inches from the back of his head*—and Sirhan never got closer than *four feet in front of Kennedy*. Sirhan's lawyers have been attempting to reopen the trial on the strength of this but need an alternate theory of the assassination. My dream suggests that another gunman, armed with a .22-caliber rifle, fired the fatal shot through a grating, perhaps overhead.

Sirhan, who had been practicing automatic writing shortly before the assassination, does not remember how he got into the kitchen hallway nor does he recall the actual events of the murder. Although he was visibly firing bullets into Kennedy and several others in the crowd with a .22-caliber revolver, the laws of physics still hold—a bullet cannot change direction.

Some might object that Kennedy was not expected to go through the kitchen passageway and the assassin(s) would not expect him there; present theory is that Sirhan encountered him there by chance. But that alternate way out of the Ballroom seems to have been used by a number of people after giving talks there. For instance, the actress Shelley Winters gave a Kennedy campaign talk in the Ballroom on June 2, 1968, and left by the same route that Kennedy took. Ominously, she felt "terrible vibrations" as she went through the kitchen passageway, and told a policeman that "something is going to happen to Bobby." She sent Kennedy a telegram asking him to be "extra careful."

On May 28, a few days before, prophetess Jeane Dixon also gave a talk at the Ambassador's Ballroom and also left via the kitchen passageway where she says she sensed Kennedy would be killed.

On that same day in Germany, I gathered all the impressions that might possibly apply to my premonition and sent them to the Society for Psychical Research in London and to Dr. Stanley Krippner, director of the Maimonides Dream Laboratory in Brooklyn, since I knew of his interest in dreams and synchronicity, especially the presidential death cycle. I summarized for him the key elements of the premonition, of which some proved right and some wrong, and added this:

> I somehow doubt if Kennedy would pay any more attention to a warning than did his brother. Even, in a curious way, Kennedy seems to be playing the role of an ancient cult god and will perhaps seek a final fulfillment of that role in a martyred death.
>
> If you can think of any way of drawing his attention to such a threat . . . I would be appreciative. If it happened, I think I should have it on my conscience; if it doesn't, then I only need feel a bit foolish.

Death struck Kennedy before a warning could have been passed on to him, but I had heightened a dilemma of parapsychology. That dilemma was succinctly put by Charles Honorton, a research associate of Dr. Krippner at the Maimonides Medical Center. His letter of June 6, 1968:

> Dear Mr. Vaughan,
>
> Stanley Krippner showed me your letter of May 28, shortly after receiving it on the morning of June 4. For some time now, I have been concerned about the dilemma we face as parapsychologists. The dilemma is a rather obvious one: if *we* take the phenomena we are dealing with

at all seriously, do we not have an ethical obligation to act on presumptive precognitive reports such as yours? On the other hand, given the complete lack of methods for differentiating between psi-mediated and "normal" experiences, how dare we, at this time, justify what in most cases would be false alarms?

This is the question I posed on the afternoon of the 4th, to a parapsychological colleague from Durham, N. C. I have no answer, nor did he. Until we are better staffed and financed as a field, it is unlikely that we will learn enough about the phenomena to feel sufficient assurance to act in similar situations.[3]

Sincerely yours,
Charles Honorton
Research Associate

What was my own reaction to the news of that tragic shooting? June 5, 1968, shortly after 11:00 A.M., my landlord interrupted my reading to exclaim excitedly in German that Robert Kennedy had been shot and severely wounded. Even though I had been fearing it, I was completely taken by surprise. Anguished grief flooded over me, and I fought a deep sense of guilt welling up from within—as if my premonition of that tragedy had been somehow partner to it. A little after noon a shudder passed through me, and I knew that Robert Kennedy was dying.

That afternoon I went to the Institute and discussed the dreams with Professor Bender. Still haunted by my own guilt feeling, I suddenly recalled words I had read that morning in Martin Ebon's *Prophecy in Our Time:* "The hero must die! Do men live out the symbols that they have created of themselves? And do their dreams, therefore, anticipate their destinies, often with striking accuracy and detail? Or do their fears and wishes communicate themselves to others who thus become prophets?"

"What will be Sirhan's fate? Could it be foretold by synchronistic links with another assassin?" Those were questions I asked myself as Sirhan's trial for the assassination of Robert Kennedy began. I looked through the records of assassination: Charles Guiteau, assassin of President Garfield . . . no; Leon Czolgosz, assassin of President McKinley . . . no; but then, there he was—John Schrank, who attempted to assassinate another presidential candidate of another famous family, Theodore Roosevelt.

In 1912 Theodore Roosevelt was again running as a presidential candidate, trying to make a comeback. Roosevelt had served out the unexpired term of assassinated President McKinley, had been elected to a full term, and was then succeeded by William H. Taft in 1909. On October 14, 1912, as Roosevelt was leaving Milwaukee's Hotel Gilpatrick on his way to deliver a campaign speech, a shot rang out from the crowd. Roosevelt was only wounded with a fractured rib. A chance coincidence had saved his life: the bullet traveled through his metal spectacle case and 100 sheets of his folded speech, which Roosevelt, undaunted, managed to read later that night despite the bullet holes.

The man who fired the revolver shot, John N. Schrank, claimed visions had urged him to assassinate Roosevelt, whom he blamed for McKinley's assassination.

Synchronistic parallels seem to link Schrank and Sirhan in an archetypal pattern of assassination:

• Both shootings took place at night at a hotel during campaigning for the presidency.

• In both shootings the weapon was a revolver.

• Both victims made a speech the night of their shooting.

• Both assailants were immigrants, Schrank from Germany, Sirhan from Jordan.

• Both Schrank and Sirhan were unusually short, and both were bachelors.

• Both Schrank and Sirhan were loners. Schrank said: "I

never had a friend in my life." Sirhan said: "Sirhan means 'wolf,' and I became more and more of a lone wolf."

• Both Schrank and Sirhan were tackled by football players immediately after the shooting, narrowly escaping being lynched. Provocatively, one of Sirhan's tacklers was *Roosevelt* Grier.

Even the very names of Schrank and Sirhan are similar, having five common letters. But already credulity is strained by the search for synchronicities—if indeed these coincidental parallels are. The test for that lies in the future, in the final fate of Sirhan Sirhan. If this pattern of assassination is prophetic, then his fate should correspond to Schrank's.

Schrank's trial was stopped when a Milwaukee sanity commission concluded that he was psychotic, or as we would say now, paranoid schizophrenic. Schrank spent the rest of his life in mental institutions, dying at the age of sixty-seven in 1943.

Sirhan's jury and judge sentenced him to die in the California gas chamber. However, recent enactment of a California bill to outlaw capital punishment makes it virtually certain that Sirhan will never enter that chamber but will spend the rest of his life in confinement.

If the parallel goes further, it may even be shown that like Schrank, whose bullets were nonfatal, Sirhan's bullets too were nonfatal—that is, the fatal bullet fired from behind Kennedy's head was fired by someone else.

In October 1972, Sirhan's lawyers appealed to the U.S. Supreme Court for a new trial on the grounds that ballistic evidence shows that Sirhan could not possibly have fired the fatal shot. Finally, in February 1973, the Supreme Court rejected the appeal without comment. There may have been a technical hitch since the evidence had not been registered beforehand with the California Supreme Court. Will there be further appeals and a new trial? Or will the evidence be squelched as effectively as it was in the case of James Earl Ray? Very likely we have not heard the end of the case.

The recent assassination attempt on the life of Gov. George Wallace has aroused speculative fear that political assassination is becoming an American way of life. Are we doomed again and again to witness more fulfillments of the archetypes of assassination?

My answer is that so long as America insists on making heroes of many of its politicians, investing them with public-relations glamor, and worshipping them as semidivine, "charismatic" personalities, then we will threaten them with the hero's fate—assassination. For it takes two to make an assassination: the victim, who invites it by yielding to temptation to become a hero; and the assassin, whose often disturbed mentality sees a way to assert his thwarted masculinity against the hero-father figure. The phallic qualities of a pistol symbolize very well the assassin's sexual inadequacies that are compensated for by the slaying of his victim. Nor is the assassin in America thwarted from easily obtaining firearms.

Many psychologists who have investigated the psychology of assassins feel that the schizophrenic tendencies (or downright paranoid schizophrenia) displayed by the assassins focuses on destroying father figures because of parental rejection in early childhood, especially by the father. Repressed homosexuality, perhaps linked with this parental rejection, seems to play a strong role in schizophrenia: the potential assassin walls off this terrifying aspect of himself into a seemingly separate mental entity that can assume many guises that provoke the assassin to murder. There is still no cure for schizophrenia nor even a complete understanding of what causes it, so at present there is little hope of curing potential assassins before they murder.

If political assassinations are to be prevented, then it rests upon the potential victim to realize that by letting himself fulfill the archetype of the hero (who must die), he becomes an accomplice in his eventual martyrdom. As soon as his political supporters begin to speak of his charisma, as soon as fans begin to reach out to touch his body or take away a souvenir of clothing, then he had best remember how to act like a mere human, not a hero of a cult.

Few people have been so touched by assassination as Senator Edward Kennedy, whose family is continually haunted by the possibility that he may join his brothers as a victim of assassination. Yet it seems to me that his unconscious mind seems to have taken in very well the gist of the above paragraph. His involvement in the drowning of Mary Jo Kopechne at Chappaquiddick may very well have sprung from an unconscious urge to avoid being placed on a pedestal. For there is no surer way to defeat the archetype of the hero than to show human failings. If his image is that of a mere man, like the rest of us, then he no longer becomes the target of the assassin.

What of the president elected in 1980? Will he be able to cheat the presidential death cycle? Will the curse of the Shawnee Prophet still hold?

Since any answer must be a prophecy, I will make this one: The curse has run its course. Even now the American Indian is demanding his full rights as a fellow American. If allowed once more the dignity of his ancient race, then he will perhaps have vanquished the spectre of the Shawnee's curse. If I seem overly partial to this explanation, it may be because I too have American Indian blood.

Moreover, I have a feeling (psychic perhaps) that by 1980 the election rules for presidents will be changed so that terms will run for five or six years and be nonrenewable, so that the next presidential election after 1976 will be in 1981 or 1982. So perhaps by a technicality we shall see an end to the archetypes of assassination.

4

The Central Premonitions Registry

The Central Premonitions Registry (Box 482, Times Square Station, New York, N.Y., 10036) was founded in June 1968 by Robert Nelson with the help of Dr. Stanley Krippner shortly after they had discussed the premonition I had sent of Robert Kennedy's assassination. A few months before they had listened to the British psychiatrist J. C. Barker lecture on the progress of his Premonitions Registry in London designed to register premonitions and possibly even prevent predicted disasters.

Also, in a less ambitious but scientifically commendable way, the CPR offered itself as a clearinghouse for registering predictions of any sort in an ongoing study of precognition. So that there could be no doubt of a prediction's fulfillment, the CPR asked that the predictions, if fulfilled, be capable of documentation in newspapers or other media. The success of the CPR has been described in detail by Greenhouse;[1] but let me give here a few examples of my own contributions to the CPR that might illustrate some of the psychological patterns that underlie prophecy.

Since it was necessary that a fulfilled prophecy be documented by a newspaper, why not try to foresee an actual newspaper headline and try to approximate a date? The method I used for this was meditation. I would sit relaxed, clear my mind for a few minutes, and then wait for an image or words to come. I would generally fix a "target date" before I started the meditation, but this did not always stay so neatly in place. Since I regularly read *The New York Times*, I selected it as my "target paper."

On March 31, 1969, I meditated on what the *Times* would say on April 13, and sent it to the CPR: "I tried to see headlines of *The New York Times* for April 13th, but later it seemed to be June 13th. There seemed to be three lines in a banner headline and a large picture centered underneath. The words came to mind: Accord Reached in Paris Talks. American Troops to Be Withdrawn in Stages from Vietnam."

Four days before my final target date, on June 9, the *Times* ran this three-line banner headline with a large picture centered underneath of President Nixon and Mr. Thieu: "Nixon to Reduce Vietnam Force/Pulling Out 25,000 GI's by August 31/ He and Thieu Stress Their Unity."

My unconscious seemed to have selected one of several possibilities current on March 31 and estimated how long it might take before fulfillment. Note that I was not actually "reading" the future headline; I only approximated it. If any of you have been impressed by mentalists on television predicting exact headlines, be assured that this is a trick known to most magicians and has nothing to do with ESP. My correctly estimating the newspaper's makeup could, of course, be put down to a knowledge of the newspaper's makeup practices, but these vary sufficiently to keep one guessing.

On December 17, 1969, I had another try at this technique, this time trying to zero in on January 2, 1970. My meditation imagery as sent to the CPR went like this: "Bells in England and perhaps other foreign countries tolling for a funeral. A photo of a carriage being drawn by horses. . . . Someone was wearing a tall, black hat. . . . *The New York Times* will print a story early in the new year about the funeral of a great foreign dignitary, a man who was known around the world. On the front page a photo . . . a horse-drawn carriage."

It was on December 22, however, that I seemed to find a close correspondence to this imagery in the *Times*. On the front page was a horse-drawn carriage driven by a man wearing a tall black hat. This had nothing to do with a funeral, but as I slid that page away from the paper to cut out the photo, I noticed showing through from the back sheet a photo with an obituary for Gen. Georges Catroux, who had joined General de Gaulle in England during World War II to form the Free French Forces.

So here my unconscious seemed to be telescoping unrelated images into a logical association. I had also—and this is very common indeed—exaggerated the importance of the event, thinking it might be someone like Harold Macmillan.

An earlier attempt had also elements of confusion. This meditation imagery was sent to the CPR on October 23, 1969: "In early to mid-November, perhaps about the 11th, there will be an international incident that will remind people of the Gulf of Tonkin incident. This may have to do with Russian aircraft attacking a base or American-based ship in coastal waters of the Far East. Also, I had an image of the ship firing back."

On November 10, the *Times* reported that in the coastal waters of the Sinai Peninsula, Russian-built destroyers from Egypt shelled an Israeli base and Israeli jets counterattacked. "The ships . . . fired at the jets." So the basic situation of the ship-aircraft incident in coastal waters was correct, but the nationalities were wrong. To confuse things, on November 11, an American base in Vietnam was attacked. Although such incidents in the Near East are now commonplace, there had been little such activity prior to that incident reported on November 10. And so perhaps it was natural that I should have superimposed on it the more familiar Far Eastern conflict.

Actually, this type of substitution—the more familiar for the less well-known—is almost axiomatic in the operation of ESP, whether telepathy or precognition. Memory traces of previous events are activated by association with similar events of the future. Totally new information, such as names or places one has never heard of, are extremely rare in ESP impressions.

One difficulty in trying to establish evidentiality of precognition in newspapers, however, is that they tend to print the same type of news on their front pages. And so I abandoned the idea of trying this method any further with newspapers.

I did send in one other prediction about a newspaper, but that appeared in a dream during an experiment at the Maimonides Dream Laboratory and it seemed to involve the Central Premonitions Registry. The dream, recorded on April 18, 1969, was part of a very long dream that seemed mainly to be about the future. I did not send it to the CPR until March 30, 1970, when I was going over the transcript: "My prediction is that *The New York Times* will do an article about the Central Premonitions Registry. A photo will accompany the article. Here is part of the dream from April 18, 1969:

"It was as though I were suddenly thrown into the future and from the future was trying to precognize something still farther in the future, and at that moment I was reading a London *Times*; a photograph was included with the article . . . I worked with some organization which had sort of caught on—enough to have been printed in the paper, and it had something to do with psychic things."

As it turned out, the fulfillment came neither in *The New*

York Times (as I predicted) nor the London *Times* (as I dreamed), but in the *International Herald Tribune* (which is made up partly from *The New York Times* international edition) that I saw while in London in September 1972. Dated August 29, it was a reprint from a *Wall Street Journal* article of August 22 on the Central Premonitions Registry. It carried a photograph of Dr. Benjamin Spock, about whom a prediction was listed. It also mentioned me. The dream image of "from the future was trying to precognize something still farther in the future" seems to correspond with the fact that a number of predictions are given in this article, about which I had dreamed nearly three years before. The probable reason for my dreaming about the London *Times* is that when I lived in London in 1967–68 the *Times* was my regular newspaper; my trip to London in September 1972 was my first return there, and I switched allegiance to the *International Herald Tribune* for that stay.

At the time of the dream, April 1969, nothing had been published about the Central Premonitions Registry, although certainly both I and Mr. Nelson hoped there would be, since a key to the Registry's success would be in letting people know about it. It was likely, then, that this interest in such an article was the trigger for the precognitive information in the dream. The connection with London seems unusual enough to take it out of the realm of conscious logic.

Altered states of consciousness, such as in meditation and dreams (which are discussed later), provide the overwhelming majority of spontaneous ESP experiences. A related state, hypnosis or trance, has also proved helpful in gaining access to the unconscious mind from which ESP seems to come. In November 1969, while doing research for an article on the mind researchers R. E. L. Masters and his wife, Dr. Jean Houston, I had an opportunity to be a subject in their Witch's Cradle, or Altered States of Consciousness Induction Device

(ASCID). The cradle is designed on a principle from the Middle Ages when witches were suspended in large sacks from trees to swing until they entered an altered state of consciousness in which they would "visit the Devil." In the modern device, the blindfolded subject is strapped upright in a swing suspended from a universal joint so that the motion of his own body rocks him into a trance (or whatever particular state he happens to enter). In my case, I seemed to enter into a light hypnotic trance.

I told Mr. Masters that I was interested in prophecy, and so he cooperated by asking me questions to which I made prophetic replies. I sent a summary of these to the CPR on December 5, 1969. What was of particular interest to me was the way that I found myself replying to the questions. Memories of previous predictions came up if I had formerly thought on the subject; fragments of things I had read seeemed to appear; half-remembered reactions to various news reports returned and assumed a prophetic form; and also some completely new information came to mind that I could not trace in the past. So it seemed to be a very mixed bag indeed.

Here are all the predictions:

1. *A madman will attack the Pope in an attempt to kill him early next year.* As it happened, a madman, as he was described in the press, made an attempt on the Pope's life the following November. I had not previously thought about the Pope, but Mr. Masters thought I said that the Pope would be killed, so perhaps this was on his mind and I picked it up, either telepathically or even logically, and then softened it to "an attempt."

2. *The President of Brazil will be thrown out of office . . .* Oops. That was a memory of an event a few years ago.

3. *Mrs. R will die in three months.* Mrs. R is still very much alive, though at the time she had been in ill health. The logical

mind seemed to carry present knowledge to a possible, but wrong conclusion.

4. *Jacqueline Kennedy will be estranged from Onassis by her son John and will take up permanent residence in the United States.* I had read of John's resentment against his stepfather and again logically carried through a possibility. I felt that Mrs. Onassis was too fond of New York to stay long in Greece, and indeed, she does seem to spend a great deal of time in New York, where she keeps an apartment.

5. *Ethel Kennedy will not remarry.* I had read rumors that she might marry the singer Andy Williams, and my instanteous reaction was, "No, she is too devoted to the memory of Robert Kennedy." Those rumors of marriage have since died down.

6. *Ted Kennedy will suffer more tragedies in the next few years but, by overcoming them, will gain the confidence of the American public to be elected president in 1976.* Shortly after Robert Kennedy's death I had two dreams about Ted Kennedy that indicated that he would one day be elected president and would be able to carry out successfully some plans laid down by President John Kennedy. As for the year, I had already concluded that President Nixon would follow the pattern of President Eisenhower and thus be elected for a second term in 1972. Therefore 1976 seemed the likely year for Ted Kennedy's candidacy. So this prediction was a combination derived from dreams, a study of synchronistic patterns, and logic.

7. *In 1970 there will be a meeting of the world's top economic leaders in an attempt to avert an international monetary disaster. . . . Wall Street will be severely affected.* By this time there have been a number of such meetings, and Wall Street reacted adversely to the floating of currencies and the devaluation of the dollar. I had been in England when the

pound was devalued in 1968, and had since paid some attention to the international monetary system. It seemed badly out of kilter, and so I would consider this a logical prediction.

8. *The Vietnam War will be substantially over in 18 months. Only a small token force of U.S. troops will then remain.* If I had been right, that would have put it in the summer of 1971. But I did have a psychic feeling that summer would be the time and amended the prediction in an interview I gave in February 1971, which was published in May 1971: "After U.S. withdrawal from Vietnam by the summer of 1972, he said, 'There might be small occupation forces, but we won't be involved in any shooting.' " [2]

On schedule, President Nixon withdrew ground troops from Vietnam in the summer of 1972. A small American ground force remained until the cease-fire was signed.

To get that date, I borrowed from another of my predictions, also published in May 1971: "President Nixon's re-election in 1972 will be mainly because of his having been able to end the Vietnam War, just as President Eisenhower was elected for a second term for ending the Korean War."

So this prediction was mainly based on logical deduction from previous study of synchronistic patterns. Nixon also seemed to have synchronistic ties with Ulysses S. Grant, as I noted in a prediction registered with the CPR on November 6, 1968: "Richard M. Nixon's administration will follow a pattern somewhat similar to that of Ulysses S. Grant. (Note that both names contain thirteen letters; both men followed Democratic presidents by the name of Johnson; and of course both are Republican.) Enormous scandals in the Nixon administration will come to light probably in the second half of his administration."

The Watergate scandal would certainly seem to qualify as "enormous." I predicted further implications in the May 23, 1971, *National Enquirer:* "A financial scandal connected with Wall Street and with people close to Nixon will occur during his second term."

9. *By 1972–1973, severe flooding will affect the Eastern Coast of the United States. This will gradually worsen in some areas, particularly New Jersey.* This prediction, in one form or another, had been on my mind since 1966, when I first had psychic impressions of flooding of New York in 1972 and 1973. It was considerably overdramatized then. But as I stood in the Witch's Cradle, I saw an image of a flooding river. I sensed it was in New Jersey. This was completely new information. The first indication of the actual flooding was in the summer of 1971 when the storm Doria caused so much flooding in New Jersey that the state was named a disaster area. Flooding in New York City was the worst in ten years. But then in the summer of 1972 the worst floods in United States history hit the eastern seaboard, again caused by a tropical storm. Whole cities were inundated and several states were declared disaster areas. New York City experienced more rain in 1972 than any other year in its recorded history.

One of the worst-hit cities in the 1972 flood was Wilkes-Barre, Pennsylvania, when a river overflowed the dikes to inundate three quarters of the city. A year before I had been walking along that dike and musing how high the river would have to rise before overflowing. I did not, however, experience any feeling of disaster (as one might expect from viewing television thrillers about ESP)—it was merely intellectual curiosity.

If I have offended any seeker of thrills who wants to believe that "strange and mysterious psychic powers" are the source of prophecy, let me apologize for including some "misses" in the above list—thereby breaking a tradition set in recent years by popular writers on prophecy. My reason for doing so is to show that every thought and image coming in human consciousness has a reason for being there, whether we call it ESP, logic, memory, or whatever. Any air of mystery is merely the result of one's ignorance or forgetfulness. In a later chapter on psychic perception, I shall try to elucidate some of the psychological patterns of ESP that give us clues to how and why prophecy works—and fails.

Of the 3,500 predictions received so far by the Central Premonitions Registry, only about 1 percent have been rated as hits—that is, a strong correlation between a prediction and a fulfillment with sufficient detail to make chance fulfillment unlikely. If this rather meager success rate were due to chance coincidence, then one would expect the hits to be distributed evenly among the letter writers. But this is emphatically not the case: most of the hits come from a handful of people who consistently score ten times higher than the average. By definition, then, these people could be called precognitive sensitives.

Do not confuse their CPR scoring rate with the claims for percentage success made by or on behalf of a number of psychics who regularly appear in the mass media. The great majority of their "fulfilled" predictions are so lacking in detail that they offer no scientific evidentiality; the CPR would keep them in the miss column, not necessarily because they were wrong, but because their fulfillment is quite within the easy reach of chance.

But trying to assess the CPR by asking what percentages are hits is rather like asking a stock investor what percentage of his stocks make money. He could answer 80 percent make money and still be losing money because of bad investments with the remaining 20 percent. The question you should ask is, "Do you have any stocks that have an unusually high return rate?"; or "What percentage of your overall investments is returned to you?" With such a stock-market analogy, then, the CPR's precognitive sensitives could be likened to stocks that return ten times as much money as average stocks.

And the CPR, of course, puts more "stock" on those people with a proven record of success.

The eventual goal of the CPR is to find a sufficiently large group of precognitive sensitives whose premonitions and predictions might independently cross-check to give an early warning of some disaster that could either be prevented or at least prepared for, such as in the case of natural disasters. But it will take a great deal more study of precognitive phenomena before we can resolve the dilemma stated by Charles Honorton in the previous chapter: ". . . given the complete lack of methods for differentiating between psi-mediated and 'normal' experiences, how dare we, at this time, justify what in most cases would be a false alarm?"

A television movie called *Visions* put forward the hypothetical problems very neatly. A college professor has a spontaneous psychic impression of someone planting a bomb in a building, and tells the police. There is insufficient detail to locate the exact building, but when the bomb explodes, the police arrest the professor as a suspect. Even in the face of ESP tests that show the professor has an unusually high degree of natural ESP talent, the police remain skeptics. Only when they get some independent confirmation of statements about the bomber do they become interested in the professor's ESP. His next impression about another bombing is more detailed, giving the shape of a freeway intersection under which the bomb is planted. By dint of expensive and exhaustive aerial surveys the police pinpoint the target and remove the bomb. "I can't believe that I have actually prevented a disaster for once," says the relieved professor. (The story continues in a dramatic way more inspired by Hollywood than by parapsychology.)

A first problem, then, is getting sufficiently accurate and detailed ESP impressions and being fairly certain that they actually are ESP, not imagination. A second problem is getting the cooperation of authorities to act on this information. As the situation exists now, the police are far more likely to act on an anonymous phone call than they are to someone's presumptive psychic impression.

Perhaps the greatest problem in trying to deal with psychic premonitions is that they rarely carry an accurate sense of time. As happens sometimes, the premonition will come years before the event although the sensitive thinks it applies to the near future. A good example was given by the French psychical researcher Dr. Eugene Osty, who became director of the Institut Metapsychique following the accidental death on July 14, 1924, of the then director, Dr. Gustave Geley. Dr. Geley had been in Warsaw for a conference and took the offer of a lift in a private airplane back to Paris. Both Geley and the pilot died when the airplane crashed.

Dr. Osty, who was making a special study of precognitive sensitives, went regularly to a Madame Peyroutet, a clairvoyant whose predictions were often fulfilled. More than two years before the accident, she made her first reference to it (March 18, 1922): "You attend a dinner regularly at which only men are present. One of them will undertake a journey and will have an accident followed by death." [3] (Geley and Osty were in a club of fifteen diners.)

(April 24, 1922): "Death of one of your friends by an accident. He will fall to his death. He is a scientific man."

(May 23, 1922): "You will learn of the death of a friend through a serious accident. There will be two deaths."

(July 15, 1922): "I always see with you the death of a scientist, your friend. But what is the catastrophe. There will be two deaths."

(September 23, 1922): "Oh! Doctor, I always see near you this death by accident. It may give rise to an offer being made to you, which will change your professional career."

(January 20, 1923): "You will hear of the death of a

scientist by an accident . . . instant death. Double death, during a journey in a distant country."

(February 17, 1923): "Always an accident and the death of a scientist whom you know well. Accident and death during a departure."

(March 17, 1923): "Oh! You will hear of an accident—death from a fractured skull. I see a death which will be the cause of something like a new undertaking, a new work for you."

(April 21, 1923): "This death of a scientist is always near you! Surely, Doctor, you have no intention of going in an airplane?"

(December 1, 1923): "What sad news of a death awaits you. Accidental death from a fall. Two dead. The day when you hear of it draws near."

(March 22, 1924): "Before long you will learn of the death of a scientist whom you know well. A doctor will fall. A motor accident, or something else, far, far away, during a journey."

(April 4, 1924): "Near you there is a death, which I still continue to see. An accidental death, abroad; something like a small ship sinking."

(May 31, 1924): Accidental death of a man you know well. Death during a departure, in a foreign country."

(July 9, 1924): There will be a death which will greatly surprise you. An accidental death. A departure during a journey. Death of a scientist, which will cause a revolution in your life."

On July 19, Madame Peyroutet once more made reference to this death, but this time in the past tense—accurately. Osty had given no warning to Geley since he did not realize to whom the prediction applied. The most distinctive information—that he was one of fourteen men Osty regularly dined with—had been given on the very first sitting, more than two years before. The warning that "the day when you hear of it draws near" was given a year and a half before the accident.

But quite ironically (or synchronistically), Dr. Geley had been warned by another sensitive three months before his fatal accident. The sensitive, named Pascal Forthuny, had been sitting at his desk when he suddenly received a clairaudient warning to go to Paris to warn Dr. Geley of the approaching death of a French doctor in Poland, who would fall victim to an airplane accident. Forthuny called on Geley and told him the warning, which Geley wrote down. Then, naturally enough, Geley asked him who the doctor was. Forthuny fumbled for a moment and gave the name of a famous French doctor. It apparently did not occur to Geley, when in Poland and being offered a ride in an airplane three months later, that *he* was the one.

Would Dr. Geley have declined the airplane ride if Forthuny had accurately told him that he was the one in danger? Geley, an expert on psychic phenomena, might be presumed to take seriously the warnings of a sensitive with whom he had worked. Yet, if the next example can be compared, a sort of amnesia can develop to block out such warnings from memory.

Another man who took psychic phenomena very seriously was W. T. Stead, who edited an English journal named *Borderlands* around the turn of the century. In 1897 he published a palmist's prediction about himself: he would die at the age of sixty-three (in 1912). Stead once wrote a story about a shipwreck that claimed many lives because there were insufficient lifeboats. In the archives of the British SPR I discovered a letter that Stead had written in 1895 to one of the founding members, F. W. H. Myers. The letter warned Myers of a premonition by one of Stead's relatives that the ship Myers was to take across the Atlantic, the *Majestic*, would meet with disaster. Myers ignored the warning and safely sailed to New York on the *Majestic*. In 1911 Stead consulted the famous psychic Cheiro (Count Louis Hamon), who allayed Stead's fears that he would meet death at the hands of a mob one day. Cheiro checked out Stead's astrological horoscope and wrote him a letter saying that the only real danger to him could come in the middle of April 1912 if he were traveling by water. Another psychic sensitive whom Stead consulted told him of a troubling dream of bodies struggling in the water in some sort of sea catastrophe and related this dream somehow to Stead. Meanwhile, the captain of the *Majestic* had been transferred to a new ship that was to make her maiden voyage across the Atlantic in April 1912. And so, disregarding three warnings, Stead was one of the more than 1500 passengers who perished because of insufficient lifeboats on the *Titanic* when it struck an iceberg on April 14.

How many of you would have signed up for a sea voyage in the face of a warning such as sent by Cheiro, as celebrated in his day as Jeane Dixon today: "Very critical and dangerous for you should be April 1912, especially about the middle of that month. So don't travel by water then if you can help it. If you do, you will be liable to meet with such danger to your life that the very worst may happen. I know I am not wrong about this 'water' danger; I only hope I am, or at least that you won't be travelling somewhere about that period." [4]

One might conjecture that Stead had accepted the final chapter of his inner destiny, going to his death as impassively as John and Robert Kennedy, ignoring the warnings and precautions of others, and perhaps remembering in his final moments his own inner presentiments of death at sea. Some scheduled passengers on the *Titanic*, like banker J. P. Morgan,

cancelled their reservations. But others rushed to the opportunity of sailing on the glamorous maiden voyage of the
"unsinkable ship."

In his book *Premonitions*, Herbert Greenhouse speculates
how such a disaster as the sinking of the *Titanic* could have
been averted if premonitions registries in America and England were sufficiently operative to force a cancellation of the
sailing. But I am more skeptical about the world's captains
of commerce heeding vague premonitions. Now, if sufficient
detailed information had been available to tell them exactly
why it would sink and precisely what they should do to
prevent it, then it is possible that they might have at least
checked out possible deficiencies.

It is more likely, however, that the ships' officials, like passenger Stead, would simply have ignored the warnings since
they were already secure in their belief that the ship was unsinkable. Perhaps, even, like Stead, all the other passengers
unconsciously knew their fate and had accepted it.

Such speculations remain to be investigated by the con-
tinuing work of the Central Premonitions Registry and other
similar registries springing up around the world (Canadians
can write to: Canadian Premonitions Bureau, Box 427, Station
F, Toronto, Ontario).

A word of advice to any who might plan a registry of their
own: Predictions about particular persons are much more
likely to be fulfilled than prophecies of general events. For
most sensitives, the patterns of abstract events or events not
concerning them directly are too difficult to tune in to. Any
sort of personal contact, even through an object, is much
more likely to yield evidential results. If you want to know
which of two candidates will be elected president, for instance, the thing *not* to do is to ask a sensitive. He will have
political opinions of his own. A more likely method of success
would be to hand a sensitive an object handled by each can-

didate, but tell the sensitive nothing except: "What impressions do you get?" Without his conscious mind (and opinions) to stand in the way of his fainter ESP impressions, the sensitive will be more likely to identify the winner.

The prophecies I made in the Witch's Cradle were all in response to questions about which I might be already presumed to have an opinion. A better method there would be to write the question on a slip of paper and fold it, then hand it to the sensitive to see if he could get any impressions. It is a curious paradox that the less you know about something (or someone), the more accurate your psychic impressions are liable to be.

Psi rushes in where logic fears to tread.

5

The "Blueprint" of Life

Every human being knows his own entire life according to laws that are still to be discovered, and metagnomic subjects [sensitives] are psychic instruments of variable quality that reveal what each human being knows concerning himself without being aware consciously, or even subconsciously, that he has this knowledge.[1]

—Dr. Eugene Osty (1923)

The above statement was made by Dr. Osty after many years of experience in eliciting predictions from psychic sensitives about his own life. The sensitives seemed to be able to tap psychically an inner "blueprint" of life that furnished information about the person's future—including events of "chance," such as the accidental death of Dr. Geley cited in the previous chapter.

When I began my year-long experiment in prophecy with English mediums in 1967, I did not know of Dr. Osty's experiments of years before. However, my own results seem to confirm independently what Dr. Osty found. If I had any preconceptions of what to expect when I began having sittings with mediums, it was that events of the near future would be easier for them to predict than events of years later. But it has taken some five years of studying about fifty transcripts of mediumistic sittings to realize that this is not necessarily so. Looking back now, I can see that it was the major events of the intervening years that were correctly forecast if the events were on the positive side. Events on the negative side were generally not mentioned, perhaps being censored by the mediums.

One of my very first experiences with mediums was not planned as a sitting at all. On June 10, 1967, when I was attending Eileen Garrett's conference on LSD, hypnosis, and ESP in the South of France, I agreed to be hypnotized as a preliminary for a later experiment. This was my first experience of hypnosis, done by a Swedish doctor who had hypnotized many cancer patients so that they would feel less pain. The hypnotic induction took over half an hour and concentrated on making my whole body relaxed. At the end of this period, the doctor said I would now come back to normal and snapped his fingers. But I didn't. I felt strangely dissociated and sensed also a sort of (psychic?) energy fluctuating around my body, as if I extended my bodily confines.

I came down into the dining room and took a seat opposite the medium Douglas Johnson to whom I had been briefly introduced. He remarked that I looked dazed. I agreed that it was how I felt. I tried then to focus this fluctuating energy to clear my mind and began to feel the effects at once. At precisely this moment, Johnson began to get spontaneous psychic impressions about me.

"You are going to write a book, but in a popular style," he said.

He then described in detail my grandmother, giving her name and saying that she had bruised her face by falling out of bed. Months later I was able to verify that she had indeed fallen out of bed about that time and bruised her face. Johnson remarked that when impressions came spontaneously to him like that they were generally very accurate.

This was to me the first clue that this psychic energy field (also called psi field) might be the carrier for information about a person, including information that the person does not himself know.

Although I was not thinking of it precisely at the moment of this spontaneous reading, the thought had been in my mind for some time to write a popular book on prophecy. My trip to Europe was primarily to gather material for it. Previously I had not published anything, although I had already written a first draft of Chapter 9 on Atlantis. So, at that time, writing a book was in the "blueprint" stage of which I was consciously aware. This theme appeared constantly in the predictions of the mediums:

(June 5, 1967): "You will write a book, and another, and lots of little ones about the first one."

(June 30, 1967): "Of your writing, only the first chapter is complete."

(July 3, 1967): "Are you writing a book or something?" ("Yes.") "Your book will be a success, but you've still got to do a lot more traveling yet."

(July 7, 1967): "A book you are writing will turn out well."

(July 13, 1967): "Who is it that is an author or trying to write books? ("I am.") "You have written one or two." ("Not yet.") "Or you are going to. . . . You are going to write and it will be a success for you."

(July 19, 1967): "I feel you're going to write a book . . . and it's going to sell. . . . You're going to write quite a lot, you know."

(August 25, 1967): "It looks like books around you. . . . You ought to write on the occult or ESP."

Three of the mediums predicted that I would be writing more than one book, and a fourth, Douglas Johnson, gave some details about a second book on August 24, 1967: "I can see what looks like a doctor's office . . . this is, I'm quite sure, a psychologist. . . . But I feel that you are in some way going to be involved with him, and there's going to be some kind of collaboration. . . . It's something that might turn into a book. . . . And definitely this book is connected in some way with ESP. And I get the feeling this could be very helpful and successful for both of you. I think the man's difficulty will be to find the time. . . . He might be about thirty-five to forty or in the forties."

The theme of collaborating on a book also appeared in a sitting with Stanley Poulton on September 14, 1967:

> Have you abandoned, have you put aside something to do where writing is concerned? ("Yes.") . . . It's just as if I've put it aside, but with the intention of returning to it. This to me is a right thing again. . . . It can be put aside until I'm sure of what I'm writing there. Are you linked up with two other people in this? I want to link two other people with you, make it three of you. People that will be very instrumental in cooperating with you. . . . They seem to be aiding you, cooperating with you in it. I would very much watch for them, because I know very much that there will be a link up with a very good man in this. Helping you in the cause of interest that he has, outside of his medical knowledge, and yet cooperating with you. . . . He will definitely be in America. . . . I feel quite sure that there has been contact, but in a very casual way. More as one would meet someone at a gathering or something of this nature.

The fulfillment of these prophecies was published in 1973: a book entitled *Dream Telepathy*, by Montague Ullman and Stanley Krippner, with Alan Vaughan (Macmillan, 1973). Dr. Krippner seems to be the psychologist described by Johnson, since at the time of the sitting he was about thirty-five. I had met him and Dr. Ullman at Mrs. Garrett's conference a few months before the sitting. Poulton's reference to "medical knowledge" may apply to Dr. Ullman since he is a psychiatrist and the director of the Maimonides Medical Center's Mental Health Center. Definite plans for the book did not come into being until about four years after the sittings. Books with three authors are something of a rarity. Books with three authors about ESP are singularly rare.

Poulton seemed to have tuned in to the three-way collaboration via the "blueprint" of the writing that I had begun but laid aside to finish for the present volume. Or put another way, the medium picked up information about book one, which in turn triggered an association with book two.

At the time of the sittings, I had hoped that this book would be published by 1969. However, I was given a warning to anticipate delay by Douglas Johnson's trance personality, "Chiang," on September 27, 1967:

> Certain things that have been told you which may seem in words to be likely to take place in a matter of weeks or months could well be fulfilled in a matter of years. Therefore it is possible that the publication of the book would, if you wish to include most of the material with a final assessment, be delayed for a long time. . . .
>
> I think you will, however, in later years write some very interesting books. And you could indeed be connected one day with a firm of publishers that deal largely with scientific matters and largely also with matters pertaining to the psychic and to parapsychology in general.

In 1967 there was no publishing firm that would have met that description. However, it is a very apt description of the British publisher Turnstone Press, which was started by Alick Bartholomew in 1972. Turnstone has scheduled publication of three books on parapsychology with which I am connected. Turnstone is also publishing some "straight" scientific works, such as Cyrus Gordon's *Before Columbus*. If Turnstone Press should represent the fulfillment of "Chiang's" prophecy, then it might be synchronistic that Douglas Johnson was invited to Turnstone's inaugural party on October 5, 1972, to celebrate publication of their first book, *Jonathan Livingston Seagull*— about a seagull who receives spiritual teachings from a "spirit" gull named Chiang.

Very few predictions were given a short and definite time limit for fulfillment. But here is a prediction given by Douglas Johnson on August 24, 1967: "Oh, some friends you're going to see soon, that you haven't seen for some time. From the States." ("Do you know when?") "I think it will be in the next month perhaps; something like that." ("Do you get a feeling of the circumstances?") "Awkward . . . no, not at the moment. I think there will be two people. Whether they're husband and wife, I'm not sure. . . . And I think that one will be of Irish extraction. . . . I saw a map of Ireland, so I think they must have Irish blood. Now the very old name of Mary is coming. This might actually come with a friend."

At the time of the sitting, I thought Johnson might be referring to an Irish friend from New York, Sarah, who had promised to look me up during a planned visit to London in August. But it was not until September 13 that Sarah called; she agreed to meet my wife and me that evening at the Mercury Theater, since we had tickets for an American play series being put on by the La Mama group from New York. I had often gone to the La Mama productions in New York. Sarah was not at the theater that night as promised, but we did meet another friend from New York, Paul, a playwright. When we told him we were looking for Sarah, he said that she was supposed to have met him in Istanbul a few weeks before but did not show up.

On the second night of the play series, however, we met with both Sarah and Paul. It turned out that Sarah had been waiting in the theater bar the night before and had finally made her rendezvous with Paul, a few weeks late. Sarah now invited us to a party on September 23, and there we met her sister Mary and Mary's husband, Sean, also Irish, who had come to London from Birmingham.

The pattern of meetings in theaters continued, but now purely "coincidental." A week later, my wife suggested we attend the last performance that evening of *America Hurrah* at the Royal Court. In the lobby I met another friend from New York, Ellen Stewart, the producer of the La Mama company. As we came into the theater we chanced to meet again Mary and Sean, who had made another trip from Birmingham. We sat with them and made plans for dinner together afterwards. After the play, as we were leaving the theater, I was amused to note that an American couple in front of us had been the only other customers in a restaurant I had lunched in the day before in another part of London.

A couple of weeks later Mary and Sean came to London again, and again we had dinner together, this time by plan. Then we went to the College of Psychic Studies for a demonstration of clairvoyance by Douglas Johnson, who accurately told Mary that she was changing art teachers. Mary was introduced to Mr. Johnson, though I did not realize at the time that she was the friend he had predicted for us.

An underlying pattern in the fulfillment of Johnson's prediction had been meetings in theaters, and the pattern continued after the initial fulfillment of meeting two people from the States, one of whom was Irish, in the month of September. The name Mary came in friendship because of the initial meeting with Sarah in the theater, and once again we met Mary in the theater, perhaps synchronistically rather than by chance coincidence.

This clustering of meaningful coincidences suggests the operation of an archetype in my "blueprint" of life. Once the archetype (the meeting of friends in a strange land) is initiated, it tends to repeat itself. Although the scene of the meetings—a theater—was not mentioned by Johnson, it may be that his brief experience as an actor when a youth has attuned him to events connected with theater.

That was one of few events forecast for the near future with a definite time. More often general themes appeared that took years to fulfill. My initial idea in collecting predictions from different mediums was that there might be cross-correspondences in the predictions so that I would be able to piece together the fragments into a more comprehensive whole. If I had similar predictions from several mediums then I could be more confident that there was a correspondence with a future situation.

One thematic series began on June 30, 1967: "Are there any connections with California, because I was being shown the Golden Gate. It would be with someone you have been involved with rather than yourself. Remember I spoke about the writing; I am speaking of writing not just as an interest or a hobby, I am speaking of bringing it into your work pattern."

I noted mention of California in the predictions of five other mediums:

(July 25, 1967): "You might go to California in something connected with your work."

(July 27, 1967): "You could be moving about rather quickly . . . California."

(July 28, 1967): "You will move somewhere where there is a tropical atmosphere . . . California."

(August 24, 1967): "Towards the end of 1968 you will go to Northern California on an assignment from a paper or journal."

(September 14, 1967): "You will be based in New York and then you will go to California for an indefinite period of time."

The theme of moving to California seemed to be linked with some publication there. I had also recorded some other predictions that spoke of a publication. The most specific of them had been: (July 10, 1967): "You will sign a contract to do free-lance journalism in England at first, then in America. The publication links up with psychic science."

(August 25, 1967): "You will be commissioned to travel and you shall travel quite a lot. A magazine will send you somewhere on the other side of the Atlantic."

At the time of those sittings in the summer of 1967, I had no idea of what publication might be referred to in California. When I had traveled to San Francisco in 1965, I had been looking for editorial work in publishing, so I knew for a fact that there was no publication there linking up with "psychic science." But towards the end of 1968, when I was back in New York, I learned of a new magazine called *Psychic*. It began publication in June 1969 from its home office in San Francisco. I began writing for it on a free-lance basis, and by the end of 1969 I became *Psychic's* eastern editor. The editor and publisher, James Bolen, invited me to fly to San Francisco in October 1970 to confer on future developments of the magazine. I made additional trips there in 1971 and 1972, and in 1973 moved to San Francisco as coeditor of the magazine.

The initial symbolism on June 30, 1967, of the "Golden Gate" is particularly apt since *Psychic* magazine's offices look out upon the Golden Gate Bridge. True to the prediction of August 25, 1967, I have been commissioned to travel quite a lot to write articles and do interviews for the magazine. The predicted time of "towards the end of 1968" was significant as the time of my making first contact with the new publication.

A similar pattern of cross-corresponding predictions began on June 29, 1967, with the statement that I would be lecturing in the future. This prediction was given by five other mediums on the dates July 6, 17, 27, and 28 and August 24. At the time of the sittings, I had never before lectured nor did I have any plans to lecture. What would I talk about?

The most specific of these predictions was made by Douglas Johnson on August 24, 1967: "You'll be asked to lecture when you get back to the States. I can see you doing a series of lectures." ("Will these be in New York?") "In New York and about. I think you'll be going to Boston."

In the fall of 1969 I began a series of lectures on ESP development in Buffalo, Boston, Philadelphia, Baltimore, and New York. The invitation to lecture in Boston came at the suggestion of Douglas Johnson! Thus, on what may be a unique occasion, the fulfillment was aided by the medium.

Mr. Johnson's ability to tune in to the specifics of these lectures was undoubtedly aided by his own past experience in lecturing at a number of these same places. Once the pattern of lecturing came into my life, it was repeated fairly regularly in the following years.

A related prediction was given by Stanley Poulton on June 30, 1967: "Have you ever done anything at all with broadcasting?" ("Not for a long time.") "I said *ever*. I see you before a microphone. I feel that I am broadcasting. . . . I cannot particularly put it out of your life, indicating by that that there will be a returning to do a certain amount with broadcasting later. There will be a returning, but in a different way than the link was in the past."

I had been a regular member of a radio book-discussion panel when I was a teenager. In 1970–72 I did a great deal of broadcasting, both radio and television, on topics relating to parapsychology. So the medium correctly sensed that a past pattern (or archetype) would return in the future, but in a different way.

One theme appeared so frequently in the mediums' predictions that I began to suspect that it might be a stock prediction, like wealth and a long life. This prediction was that I would develop my own psychic ability and work in psychic matters myself one day. Although I had had a few spontaneous ESP experiences, it seemed a far cry to be able to "turn it on" at will as did the mediums.

However, Douglas Johnson invited me to his psychic development class at the College of Psychic Studies to act as a target person for the other students to get psychic impressions about. After a period of meditation on some image proposed by Johnson, the class would then wait for other impressions to come into their minds about the target person. I attended a number of these classes afterward as a regular student, though my first attempts at getting psychic impressions were not very successful.

Finally, one night when my wife and I attended a demonstration by a *psychometrist* (one who gets psychic impressions by touching an object), we became disgusted at what looked like a stage act. When the psychometrist held up an airmail envelope someone had placed on the tray, he exclaimed dramatically: "I see this crossing the ocean in an enormous jet airliner. It came from India." We suspected that the postmark had given him more than a slight clue.

Afterwards I joked about how easy it would be to give such a demonstration. Holding my wife's ring, I imitated the psychometrist's dramatic talk. But as I talked, I was startled to see images beginning to come in my mind's eye. I described a man in great detail and learned that he was my wife's deceased grandfather. It came as a shock to both of us.

Over a period of months I found that psychic impressions became stronger and less fragmentary. When I began to feel the physical sensations of a tingling in my forehead and an activation of energy in my solar plexus, then I knew that I was getting in a psychic state of consciousness—mental images and words would begin to flow into my mind. I tended to lose my own sense of ego and merge my identity with whomever I was trying to read. And since I was primarily interested in precognition, I would attempt to make predictions about the future. I had been often disappointed in the mediums' lack of detail in their predictions, so I would try to be as precise as possible.

It was with this background, then, that I attempted on May 17, 1968, to do two things simultaneously: try to assess the predictions made for me by mediums, and try to predict my own future. I had often heard that it was not possible for people to do this, but I had to find out for myself. Here are some excerpts from that transcript.

"I will be involved in giving lectures. I see going up and down the East Coast between Boston and Philadelphia." (In 1969 and 1970 I lectured at a number of cities between and including Boston and Philadelphia.)

"Because of one of these lectures, I will get involved in some activity, some plans for lectures, more lectures but with writing which may take me away from the East Coast. I see Los Angeles and somewhere to the north of that as well, on the West Coast." (A seminar I gave in November 1969 on ESP development sparked a series of weekend seminars and lectures at growth centers in the East. I was also writing articles for *Psychic* magazine at the time. I was invited to speak in Los Angeles and traveled also to San Francisco in October 1970.)

"And I see a microphone here, broadcasting . . . I suppose an interview, a talk." (A few days after my California trip, I went to Toronto to participate in a panel discussion for the Toronto Society for Psychical Research and was interviewed on two television programs.)

"There will be a magazine article though that I will be connected with. I think it may be partially about me rather than by me. It may be about several people and me, connected with parapsychology." (In February 1972 *Coronet* magazine published a condensation of Herbert Greenhouse's book on premonitions, which mentioned me and several other people connected with parapsychology.)

"I seem to be participating in some program . . . perhaps to do with dreams or meditation . . . semi-experimental or at least attempting, proving principles." (In 1969 and 1970 I participated in a program of experimentation with dreams and meditation at the Maimonides Dream Laboratory.)

"Now Mrs. Garrett seems to be in my mind and a trip back to New York. I will see her in October. A magazine, possibly her magazine, comes in here. There is some writing for me but sending this writing out to apparently another publication. . . . Perhaps the writing is about her." (I saw Mrs. Garrett unexpectedly in October 1969. In the October 1969 issue of *Psychic* magazine, which filled out subscriptions of Mrs. Garrett's discontinued *International Journal of Parapsychology*, I contributed an article on mediumship in England, which mentioned Mrs. Garrett.)

"A lecture-writing tour . . . zigzagging perhaps to various places. There is a strong connection with a book at this point and a contract for a book." (In the spring of 1972 I "zigzagged" to the cities of Philadelphia, Dayton, Cleveland, San Francisco, Los Angeles, San Francisco, Chicago, and New York while doing radio and television publicity for Greenhouse's book, *Premonitions*. Shortly afterward I got a contract for this book.)

I should mention that at the end of that self-reading I was so exhausted and nervous that I vowed never to attempt to do it again. Although it was for me a purely experimental endeavor, I found it very, very difficult to keep out my own conscious mind. Yet I was able to tap an inner level of consciousness that knew more about my future than my conscious mind. Although I got no dates, except the mention of October in connection with meeting Mrs. Garrett, I had the feeling at the time of the reading that the predicted events might be fulfilled within a year or so. But it has taken more than five years for their fulfillment. Indeed, there were other predictions that I now realize may take many years more for fulfillment, if at all. And that applies as well to the prophecies made by the mediums.

Could I have self-fulfilled all these predictions? I must admit I certainly tried. At the time of the predictions, May 17, 1968, I had published nothing but had strong aspirations for doing so. Unpublished but aspiring authors are not exactly a rarity, but still aspiration is the first step to publication. The second step is finding someone who wants to publish one's writings. For me, that meant waiting a year until *Psychic* magazine began publishing in June 1969; once it appeared, then it was up to me to fulfill the rest of the prediction. So, certainly, the fulfillment rested in part on other people's actions in the future.

Precognizing the magazine article partially about me, having to do with parapsychology, suggests the preexistence as "blueprints" of a whole series of events over which I had no control: (1) dreams on May 25, 1968, of Robert Kennedy's assassination that were so vivid that I wrote several parapsychologists warnings; (2) Kennedy's assassination, plus my letter to Dr. Krippner, led to the formation of the Central Premonitions Registry by Robert Nelson; (3) the CPR was sufficiently successful for it to be written about in a book; (4) the book was condensed for a magazine article.

A partial fulfillment of this same prediction had occurred earlier, in November 1969 when *This Week*, a Sunday supplement carried by many newspapers, published an article on premonitions by Ted Irwin, a prominent free-lance science writer. The article mentioned me briefly but had several inaccuracies about which I wrote Mr. Irwin. I knew his address since I had been in his apartment many times in 1965 with his step-daughter, who was a close friend. At that time, I was once invited to dinner to show Mr. Irwin my first attempts at writing. He encouraged me to keep on with it and recommended that I send an article to an editor he knew at *Coronet* magazine—which was later to publish Greenhouse's article. This seemed more synchronistic and ironic when I learned that Mr. Irwin did not realize he had been writing about someone he knew. He had done research for his article in England and assumed that the Alan Vaughan mentioned in connection with the British Evening Standard Premonitions Bureau was someone else who lived in England.

Once again the Clockwork Kerass seemed to be moving in its strange elaborate ways of synchronicity. The predicted event was fulfilled in a maze of interconnecting coincidences, as if my inner "blueprints" interconnected with those of many others. It was a pattern I had seen again and again: a series of coincidences involving the fulfillment of a predicted event.

I wondered if there might be a common cause, some transcendental plan of life that preexists and guides our individual destinies. Jung spoke of synchronicities clustering around an archetypal situation. But perhaps he was only noticing particularly emotional or important (to the person) situations that exhibited more of these coincidences than average situations. Certainly the definition of archetype blurred in my mind as I studied events. Everything, in some way, was archetypal. There was nothing really new under the sun.

From the angle of the individual, his own inner "blueprints" might incorporate countless archetypal situations, many different archetypal roles—the father, the warrior, the hunter, the lover, and so on. Certainly in my case the predicted events had greater than usual emotional significance, and more coincidences clustering around them than usual. And in the background there seemed to lurk some general patterns of life that hooked them all together. In my life, then, these general patterns that tended to repeat were my individual archetypes that made up my individual "blueprint" of life. Some writers have referred to this inner "blueprint" as the *superconscious* level of the psyche, to distinguish it from repressed and forgotten memories of the subconscious. The superconscious would seem to be the source of prophecy—and perhaps life itself.

6

Psychic Perception

Nearly a century of psychical research has produced an embarrassment of riches when it comes to theories of how psi operates. (The term *psi*, short for *psychic phenomena*, is increasingly favored by parapsychologists for the phenomena of telepathy, clairvoyance, precognition, and psychokinesis since it implies no particular theory as does the term *extrasensory perception*.) My own theory is derived in part from parapsychological researches and in part from my own experience in trying to account for certain recurring patterns of psychic perception among psychic *sensitives*—people who can, more or less at will, enter into an altered state of consciousness that favors psi impressions.

There is much evidence that people and things continually emit psychic energy, which can be translated by psychic sensitives into information about the past, present, and future. A person can psychically *charge* an object by touching it, and this resultant energy transfer can be read by a sensitive.

A good example of what can happen when a sensitive is handed a sealed envelope containing a target object was given at the Parapsychology Foundation Conference at Le Piol, France, in June 1967. When the medium Douglas Johnson was handed such a sealed envelope with a picture inside, he accurately described the picture in minute detail. No one in the room knew the contents of the envelope. When the medium Eileen Garrett was handed a similar target, she described the person who had handled it recently, and accurately predicted that the person would be going to a conference in a certain city at a certain time.

Many similar examples of psychometry (or object-reading) can be found in experiences of almost any psychic sensitive. Generally, the more emotional the psychic charge on an object, the more success the sensitive will have. Other people can also serve as "objects" impregnated with psychic energy fields from a target person. Typically, when one goes to a psychic sensitive for a reading, the sensitive will be able to describe friends and relatives, both living and dead, sometimes including information about them not known to the sitter. This information can be drawn from the past, present, and future.

The quality of information that sensitives derive from an object belonging to a person will often be enhanced if the person is present as well. This suggests that the sensitive may be using the object as a means for finding psychic rapport with the person. A crude analogy might be made with holography, in which lasers are used to record a three-dimensional scene. To the naked eye, the hologram (laser pattern) has no "picture" as does a photographic negative. But when a laser shines through the hologram, the picture is reproduced three-dimensionally in space. If the hologram is broken into many pieces, each piece is capable of reproducing the whole picture, but the smaller the piece, the fuzzier and less distinct the image. By this analogy, then, the sensitive would get a fuzzy picture by holding an object of a person; but if the sensitive is able to tune in to the main psi energy field of a person, like the complete hologram, the information becomes more detailed and accurate. A person's "psychic hologram" contains an incredible amount of information, analogous to the physical information contained by the RNA-DNA molecules. Whereas the RNA-DNA molecules contain the *physical* "blueprints" of life that govern our physical development, the psi energy field would seem to contain the *psychic* "blueprints" of life that govern our inner states and development.

Some sensitives are able to perceive visually this ordinarily invisible psi field around a person or object, and term this fluctuating energy field, when visible, the *aura* or *surround.* Eileen Garrett has described how she was aware of the aura since childhood:

> I saw people, not merely as physical bodies, but as if each were set within a nebulous egg-shaped covering of his own. This *surround,* as I called it for want of a better name, consisted of transparent changing colors, or could become dense and heavy in character—for these coverings changed according to the variation in people's moods. I had always seen such *surrounds* encircling every plant, animal and person, and therefore paid less attention to the actual body contained within. . . . From their tone and color, I could tell whether a person was ill or well, and this was equally true of the plants and animals. . . .
>
> It was always hard for me to understand what my elders meant by the word "personality," because to me the secret of personality was revealed externally and physically through the blended lights of the nimbus-like covering, and it was from this that I caught impressions.[1]

Another medium who sometimes sees auras is Douglas Johnson. Once, when another medium was giving him a sitting, Johnson says that he was able to see the medium's aura expand as the medium entered a psychic state. The medium's aura then seemed to draw from Johnson fiber-like flashes into itself, suggesting that the psi field can act both as a transmitter and receiver of psi information.

Once psychic rapport between two people is established, then physical distance between them seems to be no impediment to the transfer of psi information. This indicates to me that psi fields are capable of piercing another dimension to bypass space and time. (Chapter 8 will discuss this further.)

Historically, the theory of the psi field can be traced back to about 400 B.C. to the ancient Greek philosopher Democritus, whose atomic theory has been shown by modern chemistry and physics to be closest to the truth of ancient philosophic speculations. Extending his atomic theory to explain psychic dreams, Democritus held that objects of all sorts and especially people continually emitted what he termed *images*—particles on the atomic level that carried representations of the mental activities, thoughts, characters, and emotions of the persons who originated them. "And thus charged, they have the effect of living agents: by their impact they communicate and transmit to the recipients the opinions, thoughts, and impulses of their senders, when they reach their goal with the images intact and undistorted." The images "which leap out from persons in an excited and inflamed condition yield, owing to their high frequency and rapid transit, especially vivid and significant representations." [2]

Democritus' view is in accordance with modern observations that strongly emotional situations promote the most common and accurate transfer of psi information. Soviet parapsychologists report that they have discovered a new energy field that issues from the human body—biological plasma or bioplasma—that responds to mental states. A Soviet method of radiation field photography (so-called Kirlian photography, after its inventor) has attracted a great deal of attention among American parapsychologists as a way of making visible these otherwise invisible fields. Some American scientists have equated the bioplasmic fields with the aura as described by sensitives.

Experiments by Dr. Thelma Moss and Kendall Johnson at the University of California at Los Angeles's Neuropsychiatric Institute clearly show that the most marked effects on radiation field photography are made by altered states of consciousness traditionally associated with psi—such as trance and healing. A number of healers were able to modify the energies of leaves such that, when they tried to heal punctured leaves, the photos showed the leaves' energy fields covering over the wounds; control leaves showed only the punctures. Undoubtedly it will take a great deal more research before such energies are clearly understood.

Such experimental investigations of energies on the atomic level may eventually lead to identifying individuals who may be particularly gifted in utilizing their psi potential. At present this can be done by an extensive series of ESP tests or, provocatively, by relying on the impressions of other psychic sensitives. In the previous chapter, I mentioned that a number of sensitives told me that I could develop my psi ability, and this finally encouraged me to try it. I can recall my shock, however, when I first heard myself referred to as a "sensitive" by Mrs. Garrett when she was introducing me to some scientists. Did she know something I didn't? In the light of six years, I would say, Yes.

One surprising aspect of going into my psychic state is the change it effects in my personality and well-being. As I remove the barriers to enable psychic impressions to come in, and also extend my psychic field to the person for whom I am trying to get impressions, I find myself becoming much more open in the conventional sense. A sort of loving feeling comes often with this, and an inner sense of well-being rises up and exudes what I might call a *charismatic feeling*.

This charismatic feeling is particularly evident when I attempt to heal someone. In part, my technique is to try to feel a tremendous sense of well-being within myself and then project this via the psychic field to the other person. A by-product of going into a psychic state, then, is a greater sense of personal well-being, as well as feeling relaxed and in tune with myself.

Another by-product of going into a psychic state is dis-orientation to the conventional time and space around me. As I become highly activated, sufficiently enough to lose my sense of ego-identity, then conventional time loses its meaning as I become caught up with extradimensional adventures in the future. I am also likely to forget where I am, so intense is that other place where my consciousness seems to dwell.

In such psychic states, my rational thinking practically vanishes as intuitive and associational thinking takes over. When I tried to go into my psychic state while hooked up to a brainwave analyzer (a device that displays four brainwave rhythms [alpha, beta, theta, delta] from eight electrodes placed around the forehead), I noticed that the rhythms from the right hemisphere of the brain began to predominate. This seems to fit in with physiological findings that the right hemisphere governs intuitional and nonrational thinking, while the left hemisphere governs logical thinking.

An ever-vexing problem in investigating psychic sensitives is that their readings can vary enormously in quality from one sitter to the next. Some sensitives, such as Douglas Johnson, explain this by analogy with wavelengths, as if each person had a characteristic wavelength band. If the sitter's wave-length is similar to the sensitive's, then the reading will be good; if the wavelength is at the other end of the spectrum, then there may be no results at all. I, too, have experienced this variability, as have most sensitives. Whether or not I like a person seems to have nothing to do with it, as might other-wise be expected. Yet, interestingly, sensitives almost always are able to read for each other. On the other hand, there are some people who almost never get good results from sensitives.

This same kind of variability extends to psi research in general and cannot be attributed to observable personality characteristics since the effect holds even when the experimenter has no direct contact with his subjects. Again, the concept of the psi field may be useful in explaining this difference. Each person seems to have a field of influence around him and his activities. For experimenter A, this field influences psi to function on a positive level; for experimenter B, the influence may promote consistently negative results. Parapsychologists call this difference the *experimenter effect*, which should not be confused with the psychologists' experimenter effect, which is based on subtle sensory cues.

Parapsychologists have long noted that emotional rapport between two people promotes good results in telepathy experiments. For example, the late British classicist Prof. Gilbert Murray excelled at telepathic experiments with members of his family. They would take turns at concentrating on literary scenes, which Murray could often identify with stunning accuracy. The writer Upton Sinclair had great success in telepathic drawing experiments with his wife. Most spontaneous telepathic experiences are between people who have a close emotional rapport. Such spontaneous experiences may also happen to psychic sensitives when friends or members of the family are in a threatening or emotional situation. But, paradoxically, when sensitives enter into their psychic state of consciousness and attempt to predict the future of someone close to them, they flounder badly. With complete strangers, however, the sensitives get their most striking precognitive hits.

Why should this be? Common sense would tell us that the more you know about a person, the better you should be able to predict his future. If precognition were based on rational inferences, this would almost surely be so. If precognition were based on gaining present information and plans telepathically and then projecting them into the future, once again, we would expect sensitives to be most accurate in predicting the futures of friends and relatives with whom they share a close rapport. But the opposite remains true: strangers are much more apt to receive accurate predictions. Some sensitives, realizing that the more often they read for someone, the less they will get, often refuse to see clients more than once or twice a year.

A key to understanding this apparent paradox lies in the difference between the rational and the psychic state of consciousness. The more a sensitive knows about a person, the more his rational mind will interfere with psychic impressions. If the sensitive knows nothing about a person, then he is forced to rely on psychic impressions for information. Genuine sensitives ask their clients not to reveal any information in conversation beyond a simple yes or no to their statements. As a sitter, one must learn to show interest in what the sensitive is saying without giving away any facts that might interfere with the psychic flow of information. In England, where mediums often receive their training on platforms in Spiritualist churches, the tendency is for them to ask the audience questions so that the individual to whom their impressions apply can affirm them for the rest of the audience. Unfortunately, this practice too often carries over to private sittings in which the mediums keep asking their sitters for confirmation of every statement. More professional sensitives tend to rely less on such guidance once initial psychic contact seems to have been established.

A sensitive's training can determine in large part the sort of information he receives. Those trained as Spiritualist mediums concentrate on getting information about the dead.

Sensitives who work with parapsychologists interested in telepathy comply with telepathic information, and in the same way, some sensitives specialize in precognitive impressions, others with tracing missing persons, and so on. A potential sensitive is shaped by his environment's demands just as persons with other native ability, such as aptitudes for music, writing, mathematics, and so on might be.

Characteristically, a sensitive who receives precognitive impressions will also get other information, present and past. So the best way of finding out whether a particular sensitive might be able to predict something for you accurately would be to first assess his comments about your past and present. If he is unable to make psychic contact—to get accurate impressions that can be verified—then it is unlikely that any predictions would be valid. Some fortune tellers, apparently lacking any psi ability, specialize in making predictions without first testing themselves by making verifiable statements about the present or past. Of course, they can never be shown to be wrong at the time they make their predictions.

The process of giving a psychic reading is somewhat like making up a story. As one talks, images begin to appear in the mind's eye. Verbal thoughts may come also (so-called clairaudience). Names or initials may identify people whom one sees in his mind's eye. The images are often fragmentary or symbolic and have to be interpreted by the conscious mind as one gets them. The impressions, once started, begin to flow as the conscious mind yields up its control. Sometimes the images are accompanied by a feeling of whether they pertain to the past, present, or future; at other times this distinction is jumbled and inaccurate. The solar plexus area often seems to be intimately involved in this process. One feels impressions there, or gets a gut feeling that something one sees is correct. The flow of impressions tends to come in spurts of a few minutes, then dries up, then returns as something else of interest flashes into the mind.

Each sensitive varies somewhat as to the type of information he gets, the way he gets it, and how he interprets it. Strongly visual sensitives may see images in great clarity such that they can sketch them. The Dutch sensitive Gerard Croiset, for instance, frequently sketches the scenes of locales where a missing person may be found. Other sensitives may primarily hear things in words, such as the English medium Ena Twigg. Generally, both visual and aural modes of perception come into play as well as less defined feelings.

In observing my own attempts at giving psychic readings, I have become aware of trying to establish certain key points of identification. What is a person's profession? Is he or she married? How many children do they have? Are their parents still alive? What countries have they traveled to? Where do they live? What are their interests? and so on. I generally find that I am most successful when the sitter and I share a number of mutual interests or have common experiences in our backgrounds. Psychological studies of psychic sensitives by Dutch parapsychologist Prof. W. H. C. Tenhaeff have shown how important these common experiences, especially highly emotional ones, can be in activating psychic impressions. Best known of Professor Tenhaeff's subjects is Gerard Croiset, who specializes in finding lost children (often drowned in Holland's canals). As a child, Croiset nearly drowned himself in a canal. Not only do these common points serve as a focus around which a sensitive builds impressions, but the memories themselves can surface as psi responses.

An analogy I often use is comparing each individual to a highly complex computer card with holes punched for each experience. Each of us throughout his lifetime undergoes many thousand experiences, with more or less vivid memories accompanying these according to their emotional impact. Assume, theoretically, that these experiences are represented in our psi fields and could be punched into a computer card, with the more emotional memories having the larger holes. Now, the sensitive also has such a computer card that he overlays on that of the person seeking a reading. By entering into a psychic state, the sensitive throws illumination on the two cards. Wherever there is a close correspondence between the two, the illumination will show through. A point of contact is made. A psychic response is triggered, sometimes the sensitive's own memory, other times more accurate information about the sitter. Once several points of contact are made, then other information flows through more easily. If this analogy is expressed in terms of psi fields, then one could say that a mutual resonance was achieved between the interpenetrating psi fields. The strongest points of resonance—the most emotional—would generally be archetypal, that is, recurring patterns of human experience.

The archetypal nature of these psychic images is revealed by the frequent appearance of symbols in the sensitive's impressions. Some symbols may be universal, such as a funeral wreath or a casket representing a death. Others may be directly derived from one's own experience. To Croiset, for instance, the symbol of a half-eaten peach means that a person has terminal cancer. Croiset's mother died from cancer after eating half a peach.

As in dreams, memory traces can serve as more elaborate symbols. For instance, once when I was demonstrating psychometry for a group and was trying to pick up impressions about a young man, I immediately thought of a previous reading I had once given to a woman whose husband, an architect, was moving to Connecticut. I asked the young man if he lived in Connecticut. No. Was he an architect? Yes.

Initially, I had grasped the "wrong end" of the symbolic association.

Sometimes the symbols are drawn from the sitter's experience. Once, when giving a European woman a reading, I got the impression that her husband had been killed during the war. Then the Russian word *chemodan* flashed into my mind. Since *chemodan* means "suitcase," I interpreted this to mean that the woman traveled at this point to another country. I was right. But she added after the reading that her husband was a Russian, and that a Russian slang use of the word *chemodan* meant coffin. In my study of Russian, I had not come across this usage. But to the woman, the word *chemodan* simultaneously evoked the nationality of her husband, his death, and her traveling.

An incident related to me by Croiset has a similar ring, except that the sitter could not interpret the symbol until many months later. The sitter was a young man who had been depressed by several work failures. Croiset saw a bright future for him, but then got the puzzling symbol of a black chicken, which neither of them could interpret. Months later, the young man answered a box number advertisement for a job and was launched into a successful career as a salesman for a liqueur called Black Chicken. In this case, the symbol had a literal meaning in the man's future.

I, too, have been surprised sometimes by how literal symbolic associations can be. Once, when reading for an out-of-work actor, I got the impression that he would be very successful. The name of the Cherry Lane Theater in Greenwich Village came to mind. I had once been there to see a play. I asked the actor if he had ever been there. No. I predicted then that he would open in a successful show at the Cherry Lane Theater. Over a year later he got a part in *Godspell*, a very successful show that opened at the Cherry Lane Theater.

Thus we both had a common association with the Cherry Lane Theater—mine in the past; his in the future.

At other times the names of people or places will assume a symbolic rather than literal quality. In trying to get impressions about a student, I saw an image of an Irish friend named Sarah. "Either your girlfriend is named Sarah or she is Irish," I said. "She's Irish," he replied. When Douglas Johnson was reading for a woman on television, he saw the image of a British penny. He interpreted it correctly as a girl named Penny, the woman's daughter.

In Holland I once gave a reading on a coin handed me by a student interested in parapsychology. I had tried unsuccessfully to pick up anything about him directly. But the coin, which was pressed into my hand so that I could not see what it was, was an English shilling sent him by his girlfriend in England. I then described the boy's girlfriend and added that I felt a tremendously powerful feeling of religion accompanying this. I worried that they might have a difference in religion as it seemed to assume such a great significance. He corrected my misapprehensions by telling me that his girlfriend's father was the bishop of a cathedral. I still, however, could not seem to pick up anything at all about the student himself. This was somewhat embarrassing as he was the president of a parapsychological group. Giving it one last try, I said; "Your mother died of cancer recently." Wrong again. But the student sitting on my other side interrupted by saying that *his* mother had recently died of cancer. I then tried, successfully, to get more impressions about the other boy. For some reason, I could not relate psychically at all to the student president of the group although I liked him personally. So it would seem that a flow of symbols can be established only when there is a certain amount of psychic compatibility. A lack of this compatibility can prove embarrassing, as when a sitter brings a stenographer with him for a sitting but the medium can get impressions only about the stenographer.

While it is true that sensitives tend to be correct when their impressions revolve around an area of special interest, it is equally true that they can be incorrect just as systematically. For instance, I have attempted at least five times to tell a pregnant woman what the sex of her child will be. I have been wrong every single time. I suspect that this psi-missing is due to the forced-choice guessing situation, which I dislike.

A common fear that many people have about consulting sensitives is that the sensitive may foretell their death. Dr. J. C. Barker, who founded the English Premonitions Bureau, felt that people so forewarned about their own death might make it a self-fulfilling prophecy. Dr. Barker and a colleague consulted a number of fortune tellers, astrologers, palm readers, and other presumed sensitives in the London area to see if any of them would forecast their deaths. Almost universally, Dr. Barker was assured of a long life, although he was warned against illness and deaths of other members of his family. In his conclusions, Dr. Barker said: ". . . it was highly probable that some of the forecasters were deliberately withholding unpleasant information that they might have been about to foresee about our health or death—we shall never know. It is significant that two of them refused to make forecasts about my death even in response to direct questioning." [3]

Dr. Barker's account of this experiment, *Scared to Death*, was published after his premature death in the summer of 1968. We might conclude that the fortune tellers either consciously or unconsciously censored any impressions about his death, since they were able to pick up other information about him quite accurately.

In former years, however, fortune tellers and palmists were less reluctant to make predictions of death. A footnote in a

French study, *La Psychologie de la Main* [Psychology of the hand] by N. Vaschide, a French psychologist, tells a grim story all its own. One of Vaschide's most gifted subjects was a sensitive named Madame Fraya, who flourished around the turn of the century. "Mme Fraya predicted to the author of this work during the winter of 1904 that he would die of pneumonia in his thirty-third year. The Countess de Noailles, who was present, Mme Fraya, and N. Vaschide himself confirmed this prediction, which, unhappily, came true October 13, 1907. A year before his death, a gipsy from Roumania told him in 1906 that he would die in the following year." [4]

That footnote, supplied by Vaschide's widow, is far less smiling than Vaschide's own comments in his book: "Formerly I used to smile when listening to the prophecies of fortune-tellers; but since I have studied these problems, I still smile at the conjectural predictions and naive affirmations of future events; nevertheless, I have verified the large amount of knowledge and psychological data that an organ so complex as the hand may furnish."

Vaschide's main conclusion, by the way, is seriously doubted today by most parapsychologists. Palmists seem to derive their most astute impressions not from the lines of the hand, but from touching the person to make psychic contact. It seems surprising that Vaschide should not have wondered what line in his hand would indicate fatal pneumonia in his thirty-third year.

An unpublished study by Brigitte Rasmus at the Freiburg University's Institute for Border Areas of Psychology showed that a number of German palmists were unable to make accurate statements about people's characters when only photocopies of the handprints were presented to them. Perhaps additional studies along these lines might finally establish what, if any, information might be derived from the lines of the hand as opposed to psychic impressions.

A similar area of difficulty to research is astrology. Although astrology's proponents are vociferous that "astrology is a science," there has been very little scientific investigation of what part an astrologer's psychic sensitivity might play in arriving at accurate character assessments and predictions of the future. Parapsychologists generally shy away from investigating such occult topics as astrology. I know of only one parapsychologist who has ventured to investigate astrology (but not so far as to publish his results). Out of twelve German astrologers who were sent "blind" birth data from a number of people, only one was able to score significantly above chance in his astrological readings, which were judged "blind" by all those whose birth data had been submitted. In his favor, the successful astrologer was able to cite specific astrological reasons for his statements. Again, many more such experiments are needed to establish what, if any, validity "scientific" astrology may have.

My own small experience with astrologers has given me the impression that their best hits are psychic rather than astrological, though in truth it is very difficult to separate the one from the other. I would say in general that astrology is more of an art than a science. Claims that astrology can be accurately programmed by a computer were put in doubt by a group of French astrological skeptics who tested the first astrology computer in France. The skeptics sent in to the computer birth data from France's ten worst criminals, who received mostly glowing accounts of their character. For a man who had been executed, the computer promised "an enriching love life." The skeptics placed an advertisement in a French newspaper promising a free astrological reading for anyone who wrote in, with the stipulation that the recipients must reply as to how well the reading fit them. Hundreds of people wrote in for their free reading, but they all received the same one—that of the executed criminal. Casting doubt on the public's ability to assess the validity of astrological readings, 90 percent of the recipients replied that the criminal's reading fit them very well. The skeptics had certainly shown that people want to hear good things about themselves, but their test was not really scientific. To put such a test on a par with parapsychological experiments, the skeptics would have had to furnish at least two readings from which to choose —one, a reading from the person's own birth data; and the other as a control. If at least half of the people chose the control reading over their own, then the skeptics would have a valid point. If the "actual" readings were chosen at a much higher rate, then the computer would have the upper hand. So, until truly scientific experiments are done with astrology computers, no valid conclusions can be reached. It seems astonishing to me that so few experiments in astrology have been attempted, since by its nature "scientific" astrology could lend itself readily to scientific experimentation. A possible explanation for this is that believers do not require scientific evidence while disbelievers do not deem astrology worthy of investigation.

Claims coming from Czechoslovakia that astrology can provide foolproof birth control information seem to be highly suspect. Cycles of a woman's fertility are reckoned from her birth data. According to Dr. Joachim Jonas, a woman can conceive during her menstrual period, which sometimes falls in the maximum fertility period according to his calculations. If this is so, then why have not other doctors noticed this same phenomenon?

To many people, however, astrology is a belief system. Moreover, like other belief systems, astrology may work for those who believe and not work for skeptics. The question remains to be answered by scientific experiments. Another belief system that dates back thousands of years in China is the *I Ching*, or *Book of Changes*. By a tossing of coins or yarrow stalks, one builds up a hexagram that corresponds to one of the sixty-four hexagrams in the *I Ching* and the corresponding reading for each hexagram. The *I Ching* appealed to Carl Jung as a basic example of synchronicity—that one's inner questions correspond with a chance throw of coins to give the *I Ching's* answer.

To test what influence belief or nonbelief might have on one's success with the *I Ching*, Lawrence Rubin and Charles Honorton of the Maimonides Medical Center in Brooklyn asked forty subjects to pose a question that had great personal meaning to them.[5] With their questions in mind (not spoken aloud), the subjects threw coins until the hexagram was built up. The experimenters then showed the correct hexagram's reading to the subject along with a control reading, randomly chosen, and asked the subject to rate from one to ten how appropriate each reading was. To rule out any possibility that the subjects might recognize what the coin throws meant, only persons not formerly acquainted with the *I Ching* were used. To include the belief factor, the experimenters asked the subjects whether or not they believed in ESP. The thirteen nonbelievers got an overall negative score. The twenty-four believers got an overall positive score. The difference between the groups was statistically significant, though overall results were not significant. If such a relationship continues to hold in future replications of this experiment, then it may at last provide scientific evidence that belief influences things. A New Testament way of saying this may be "Prayer changes things"; that is, if one believes. It should be added that one cannot believe in prayer without believing in ESP, since prayer is essentially a sending of a telepathic message to a divinity.

The *I Ching* is only one of countless methods of divination that man has used through the ages to foretell the future. Some of these systems, such as the reading of sheep's entrails or tea leaves, would seem to include a psi factor—a sensitive uses the chance pattern as an initial means of focusing his psi ability. In some cases, though, as with Tarot cards and the *I Ching*, the element of synchronicity may be introduced so that chance events take on a paranormal correspondence. No scientific experiments with Tarot cards have been published to my knowledge, so one cannot make any firm statements. My single experience with a Tarot reading was provocative: the same central card appeared in the same place in three successive layings-out of the twelve "major arcana" cards by a reader after I had shuffled them each time. The reader's predictions, though vague, seemed substantially accurate.

Far more detailed, and therefore evidential, predictions are likely to come from sensitives in a variety of modes of perception. In one series of long-distance telepathy experiments conducted by an English sensitive, Mrs. A. M. Kaulback, with her two sons, Ronald and Bill, some interesting facts emerged. In more than 250 attempts to describe her sons' activities many thousands of miles away, Mrs. Kaulback wrote out "word-pictures" that she felt came from discarnate communicators rather than her sons themselves. Both boys kept detailed diaries so they would be able to annotate their mother's impressions later. Some of Mrs. Kaulback's detailed word-pictures corresponded in both time and detail to the boys' activities; others were *postcognitive*—descriptions of recent past events; while still others were *precognitive*—descriptions of future events. Here is an example of such a precognitive word-picture that was written in England on November 4, 1942, when Bill Kaulback was in the British army in North Africa:

> I [Harry Kaulback, Mrs. Kaulback's deceased husband] want to tell you that Bill is getting command of a battalion. I am very proud of him. I was with him when he got orders

and, when you write, tell him Pop was with him when a message was handed to him.

Bill had been having breakfast and was on his way back to his own house. An orderly came up, saluted, and handed him a letter. Bill tore it open and exclaimed with pleasure. Then he retraced his steps and went into a room—evidently a study—where there was an officer. I think his rank was that of a full colonel.

Bill showed him this letter and this other man said: "I congratulate you but am very sorry to lose you."

Bill's annotation was:

> On this day (Nov. 4, 1942) the battle of El Alamein had just reached its climax and early that morning my division —the 7th Armoured—spearheaded the break-through and started the pursuit into Cyrenaica. I was then second in command of the regiment.
>
> It was not actually until a month later, on the 1st of December, that the scene occurred which is described here so accurately. It was early in the morning that a message arrived from Army Headquarters appointing me to command another regiment in the Brigade. I had been waiting for this for some time. . . .
>
> We were at Benghazi at the time in bivouac [in tents], but the Brigade Headquarters was in a building, and I went over there to see my late Commanding Officer who was temporarily in charge of the Brigade. So by chance it *was* in a room that I broke the news to him. All is exactly as Dad describes except that the officer was a Lieut. Colonel and not a full Colonel.

Thus the telepathy attempt of November 4, 1942, was an inadvertent prophecy of what was to take place a month later several thousands of miles away. This type of temporal confusion happened so often that Mrs. Kaulback asked one of her communicators, "Uvani" (who more often was the Arab control of Eileen Garrett), for an explanation. He replied through her hand that ". . . at times the pictures are perchance taken from the mind of the boy and shown to you. And it must therefore be that we strive yet more earnestly that we see but actual deeds, for thoughts are not what we endeavor to collect. Sometimes, too, the visions slip from firm grasp, and we see what is about to be done perhaps at some future date. It is not easy grasping time between two planes; and in addition do we try to grip the different times upon your earth, therefore on occasion do we sadly err."

Mrs. Kaulback's unique experiment, the story of which is being revised and expanded for publication under the title *By Request of Uvani*, contains many insights into the nature of time as experienced through mediumistic communication and also the nature of mediumistic controls or "spirit helpers." Highly emotional opinions are held on both sides of the spiritistic hypothesis, but there is no space for a broad examination of the pros and cons here. My initial reaction to the concept of a spirit controlling a medium was that, if the spirit were a truly independent agency, then he ought to be able to come through different mediums and show knowledge of previous communications through the other mediums. And that is exactly what "Uvani" did when he spoke to Mrs. Kaulback and a witness through the entranced Eileen Garrett in 1936 and expounded further on the nature of time as experienced in Mrs. Kaulback's experiment:

> You have had your pictures given in many ways, and you have recognized this: that time is not always a measureable quantity. In the beginning we limited ourselves to give you time which corresponded with that of yours, and it was noticeable that those pictures which were very small were more often correct. It was then comparatively easy to grasp the time of your boys with your time. Then came pictures on a larger canvas which were frequently incorrect with your time. The interest, however, still remains that we gave you pictures, and that actually what we saw was correct. . . . When a man takes a record he does not confine

himself to one small item. What he sees he strings together. So with us. We also wished to make clear that time is as nothing; for yesterday, today and tomorrow are one.

You have had your pictures given in many ways. There were moments when we took what passed in the minds of the boys for actual occurrences. It was taken by us at times to be the vision of what would make the concrete action later. We could not always foresee. . . .

The trance personality of Douglas Johnson, "Chiang," also expressed his thoughts on the enigma of time in mediumistic impressions: ". . . with predictions it is sometimes difficult, not only for us in our world, but also for those in the physical body who utilize their psychic ability to channel and to truly fix the time. The essence of the predictions may be perfectly correct but the time may be altered by the free-will of the individual. . . . I think that ordinary psychics in their normal state can give prophecies that are just as likely to be correct as those who are not in the physical body."

An interesting comparison between a medium's own ability at predicting the time of an event and his control's ability was afforded in a 1967 sitting given by Douglas Johnson to an electronics engineer. In the first part of the sitting, Johnson was controlled by "Chiang," who predicted that an elderly woman known to both the medium and the sitter would die in five to seven days. After coming out of trance, Johnson said he thought she would die the next morning. She did indeed die the next morning. When I asked "Chiang" about this incident after the sitter had told me about it, "Chiang" replied: "Psychics working with their own psychic ability, because they are living in their own dimension, can see forward in time more accurately than we. . . . It is easier for sensitives to forecast time more accurately on their own than in a trance state and controlled, shall we say, however remotely by us."

Certainly, my own experience with mediums and their

trance personalities would bear out that statement. If indeed, as "Uvani" said, "yesterday, today, and tomorrow are one," then it is not surprising that a sensitive living in our temporal world should have a keener sense of chronological time when predicting events.

Many sensitives report that getting impressions about the future is like remembering—only forward instead of backward. An unconscious train of thought, with the "cars" linked by associations, travels through the tunnels of the mind until it pops out into consciousness. Perhaps "remembering" the future is very much like remembering the past. Events of the last few minutes are generally easiest to recall. But if I ask you what you had for breakfast last Wednesday, you probably won't recall. If I ask you what you had for dinner on November 22, 1963, there is an excellent chance you will recall—not because it was an unusual meal, of course—but because of the emotional association of John Kennedy's assassination. Although the two events were not logically linked, they are linked by emotional association, and it would seem to be emotion that fixes memories in the mind most clearly.

This may explain why very emotional or important events can be precognized at very great intervals of time, while trivial events tend to arrive soon after the precognitive impression.

7

Dreaming the Web of Time

Dreams provide some of the most compelling evidence for the reality of precognition. Even persons who in their waking life are unaware of any psychic sensitivity can experience in their dreams previsions of the future. In the thousands of cases of spontaneous dreams reported as precognitive to parapsychologists and psychiatrists, most tend to fall into the categories of the terrible and the trival: death and disaster on the one hand, and absurdly meaningless trivia on the other. Most commonly, precognitive dreams pertain to the future of the percipient, though often in disguised or symbolic form. To attempt to make use of dreams as prophecy, however, one must learn to analyze them—to sort out past and possible future elements, to compare different dreams for their common elements, to bring to the dream one's own associations from the past in relation to events of the present in order to project possible future associations.

Pioneer experimental work in investigating precognition in dreams, such as J. W. Dunne's *An Experiment with Time*, focused mainly on the problem of accumulating evidence that dreams can contain elements of the future. No appreciable attempt was made to identify precognitive dreams beforehand, nor to analyze them beforehand for elements that might give clues as to why these dreams might be different from other dreams. Yet, occasionally, someone would send a parapsychologist a dream that he or she thought might pertain to some future event of general importance.

In one interesting case reported by the Dutch parapsychologist W. H. C. Tenhaeff, there seemed to be a (synchronistic?) mesh of events that began when Professor Tenhaeff was testing a psychic sensitive at a hospital in Amsterdam in October 1937. After the testing session, they remained at the hospital to chat with the medical superintendent and some others. Then the sensitive spontaneously told the superintendent that within a few weeks he could expect a party of distinguished people in the hospital: Queen Wilhelmina, Princess Juliana, and Prince Bernhard. Professor Tenhaeff did not take this very seriously, but he made a note of it. At about the same time, a medical colleague told Professor Tenhaeff of a woman patient who had dreams of psychoanalytic interest. Tenhaeff met with her for a consultation, and soon afterward, on November 27, she wrote him a letter about a dream: ". . . everything I saw clear like crystal so that I cannot forget it. I saw a railway crossing and a long road and pastures. Behind the gate to the left stood a truck. A car comes along at a terrible speed trying to cross at the last moment but as it crosses, a tire bursts and the car crashes at full speed against the gate and the truck behind it. The driver of the car was killed immediately. I saw his face when he was lying there, it was Prince Bernhard. . . ." [1]

Two days later, in very similar circumstances, Prince Bernhard was severely injured when his speeding car hit a truck. (He was not killed as the dream indicated, but a number of correct details put this into the class of evidential precognition.) The Prince was taken to the nearest hospital, the same one where Tenhaeff had been the month before. So severe were the Prince's injuries, that the consulting physicians advised that Queen Wilhelmina and Princess Juliana stay at the hospital for a few days with him, which they did, thus fulfilling the prophecy of the sensitive. As often happens, Professor Tenhaeff did not connect the sensitive's prophecy with the woman's dream until after the incident.

To gain insights into the nature of precognitive dreaming, one must probe beyond the correspondence of dream and future event to find underlying patterns that may tend to activate nocturnal "time-tripping." The approach used by Prof. Hans Bender at the Freiburg University Institute for Border Areas of Psychology with his star precognitive dreamer, Mrs. Christine Mylius, has been highly illuminating. For about nineteen years, Christine has been filing copies of her dreams with Professor Bender. About ten percent of the over two thousand dreams have shown correspondences with future events. Christine is an actress, and many of her precognitive dreams are about future roles in films or on the stage. Indeed, the story of how her dreams mirror her future acting roles would make a fascinating film itself.

Professor Bender has already made a short documentary film in German on one remarkable series of dreams that focuses on a 1959 German feature film *Night Fell on Gotenhafen*.[2] Christine's dreams anticipated by two years many of the key scenes of this film, which was based on a true story that happened during World War II. A Russian submarine torpedoed a ship filled with six thousand German women and children who were fleeing from the port of Gotenhafen. Nearly all the refugees were killed, though some managed to get into lifeboats. Christine plays a woman whose infant child falls into the water in the confusion; she becomes mad with grief, jumps overboard from the lifeboat when she mistakes floating debris for her lost child, and she drowns. The scene was filmed on September 15, 1959.

Exactly two years before to the day, Christine had reported

a dream in which she had been swimming underwater with an infant child. "We are playing 'meeting under water' and I am afraid because she stays down so long."

When I interviewed Christine about this case in May 1968, we noted some synchronistic episodes that pertained to the *Gotenhafen* film of 1959. On May 12, she wrote me that I would be able to see on television the following week not only her film *Night Fell on Gotenhafen* but also films in which her husband and one of her three daughters acted. The evening before, Christine had gone to a party where she met for the first time the writer of the *Gotenhafen* film script.

The actual ship on which the *Gotenhafen* movie was filmed was named the *Hanseatic*; it was pressed into movie service again for a 1966 television film *S.O.S. Morro-Castle*, directed by Frank Wisbar, who had done the earlier *Gotenhafen* film. Again, the film was based on a true story. The *Morro-Castle*, sailing from Havana to New York in the 1930s, caught fire and brought tragic death to many of the passengers. Christine was given the role of a passenger, and the director asked her daughter Angela to play her first professional role as Christine's stage daughter.

On May 8, 1966, a scene was filmed in which Christine and Angela are on the deck of the burning ship, and Angela jumps overboard. Several months before, December 30, 1965, Christine had recorded this dream: "A very stormy crossing on a small steamer . . . it's rocking indescribably . . . I want to see the play on deck. . . . Angela comes on, slips and falls in."

Not long after the *Morro-Castle* film, the ship *Hanseatic* was again featured on film as a burning ship. But this time, the film was a newsreel, and the *Hanseatic* actually burned in New York harbor, repeating in real life its role as the *Morro-Castle*.

The pattern of ship disasters underlay another series of dreams that began on December 11, 1965. Christine dreamed that her daughter, Bella, also an actress, was with an astronaut, who was locked in a capsule. "He must be freed quickly—there is a small screw cap . . . which I must remove from his windpipe so that he doesn't choke." Christine administers artificial respiration, and the man is saved. She thought it was like a film production, and commented: "Since Bella occurs in it, can it be that I have predicted a film for her?" About nine months later, Bella got a role as an astronaut for a filmed television space-travel parody.

Another element of the dream was fulfilled two days later, on December 13, 1965, at Cape Kennedy. The German newspaper *Bildzeitung* displayed the story in headlines: "Giant Scandal in Cape Kennedy." A small plastic cap had been left by mistake in the pumping system of *Gemini VI*, blocking off a fuel line—corresponding to the small cap blocking the astronaut's windpipe in the dream. But, as in the dream, catastrophe was averted and the astronauts later blasted off safely.

The space-travel film in which Bella played an astronaut was finally shown on television on January 4, 1967. In one scene Bella says the countdown for a rocket launch, which ends in a comic mishap. After watching the film on television, Christine dreamed that night that "somewhere an irreparable stupidity was happening. Something was running down like a clock 4-3-2-1 . . . it seemed as if there had been a rocket launch failure. . . . I woke again at four with the words: 'Attention rocket launch,' then dead silence, as if something had gone wrong." Christine commented: "I can have taken the film again as a cause in my dream for an actual stupidity."

Twenty-four days later, at Cape Kennedy, a simulated countdown was taking place. Three astronauts perished in the *Apollo I* capsule when fire broke out in its high-oxygen atmosphere. Investigations brought charges of gross negligence, or "great stupidity" as Christine had dreamed.

Christine has no particularly great interest in space travel, but seemed to have incorporated into her dreams the two Cape Kennedy incidents only because her daughter was to play the role of an astronaut. Christine's first dream predicted the role, and when she finally saw the film on television, it triggered the second dream, transforming a comic mishap during a countdown to one of tragedy. Synchronistically, both the series of dreams about the ship *Hanseatic* and the space ships ended with the actual burning of the ships.

When I was doing research for this chapter in May 1968 in Germany, I resolved to read through all of Christine's two thousand dreams to find out if any of them might have predicted the actual burning of ships. Somewhere in this reading I encountered two dreams about burning to death but no mention of ships, so I did not note them down. However, when I finished the research, I realized that they must have been the closest dreams to what I was looking for, but now I could not remember where they were. Would I have to go through all two thousand again? That night, May 13, 1968, however, I had a curious dream:

"I now remember a lottery I watched for a while. Everyone put down hundred-dollar or -mark bills. The croupier went through some elaborate system of writing numbers on a board which were supposed to correspond to the serial number of the winning bill. I thought I had a winning bill, but when the croupier explained the system, I had to admit that I did not. But the serial number of my bill was exceedingly close to that of the winner."

In my wallet at the time was a hundred-mark bill, the serial number of which was 0614173. I remarked: "Perhaps I shall see another number today very much like it."

The next day, I was again examining the dream records when I recalled my dream, and once again studied the serial number of the bill. If it were to correspond somehow with the dream numbers, then there were only two possibilities. Reading forward, there was 1417; and backward, 1416. I looked up the numbers in the dream books, and there were the two dreams of burning that I had sought. But this was still "not a winning number" since no ships were involved.

Three days later, I received in the mail a check forwarded from New York on the day of my dream, the thirteenth. The check's serial number began with 0613, differing by only one digit from the beginning of my hundred-mark bill's number, 0614. Indeed, I did "see another number very much like it."

Seeming to fulfill two purposes simultaneously, my dream and the serial number of the hundred-mark bill provided me with the needed numbers of the "burning" dreams as well as an example of synchronicity of numbers. I had been actively thinking about both problems just before the dream, and the dream seemed to have provided the answer.

A peculiar form of synchronicity common in Christine's life is that a dream often corresponds to an event that happens to the day one or more years later. I call them "anniversary dreams." For example, she had the following dream on January 22, 1967, when she was staying at a hotel near a train station: ". . . another woman or I had to play a *locomotive*— this must be performed and I believe I must play it then."

Playing the role of a locomotive seemed absurd. But on January 22, 1968, an actress friend asked her if she would like a role in a new play in which she herself was to act. It was entitled *Locomotive*. Christine declined the part, but her friend played the mother of a girl whose name, Bella, was the same as Christine's daughter.

Earlier, on May 5, 1966, Christine dreamed of a role she was to play and sketched the costume the next morning. Only one thing was wrong—the collar of the dress was missing. On May 4, 1967, dress rehearsal began for a new play, in which

Christine wore the dress she had sketched a year before. The collar, oddly enough, was missing, but was supplied the next day, May 5.

On May 24, 1958, Christine had a Kafkaesque dream of a department store: "With my husband in a large department store where I have first bought something, and now I have only an exchange credit voucher. I'd like to get a wool jacket. I try one one, a beige one, and it fits well. But the salesgirl slams down three too small for me, which I first took —all three are also beige—but they don't fit and I must take them back to exchange again." The dream was ostensibly triggered by an event the day before, when her daughter showed her a new beige wool jacket, which she had admired, and thought of buying one also.

On Monday, May 25, 1959, when Christine was in Italy, a male friend suggested they go to a department store to buy her a wool jacket as a return present from him for the birthday present she had given him the day before. She admired a jacket in an apricot fabric, but the friend suggested a beige one, which she bought. When she got home and tried it on, the friend pointed out that it was too small. She went back to the store to exchange it. By bizarre coincidence, the clerk made the same mistake twice more by giving her the beige jacket in a size too small. So, she ended up exchanging it three times before getting one in the right size. Exchanging beige jackets three times in one day is not the stuff of everyday coincidence.

A dream of August 8, 1961, seemed to combine elements of events one year later to the day and five years later. Christine dreamed that "Bella has an offer of work in a film . . . I myself am in Baden." She further dreamed of flying in a private airplane with her daughter Andrea. Then she found three types of edible mushrooms in a wood.

On August 8, 1962, Christine was given her first ride in a

private airplane, and her daughter Andrea also got her first ride on the return journey.

On August 8, 1966, in Austria, Christine and a cousin picked the three types of edible mushrooms in a wood. The following day, she was joined by her daughters Andrea and Bella, and together they ate the mushrooms. From there, Bella went on to start a new film engagement in Baden.

This "anniversary dream" type of synchronicity aids Christine in identifying precognitive dreams. In periodic trips from her home in Hamburg to Freiburg, she brings her diaries to compare with the dream records on file. Her first impulse in checking events is to review dreams of that same date years before. Her diaries are written in printed books that have five years arranged under each day of the year. So, for instance, when she noted in her diary on July 30, 1967, that a friend, the one who owned the airplane, died of lung cancer, she looked back through the dream records of that date. There was a correspondence with a dream of July 29, 1964, in which she dreamed of that person's death; she saw him in his airplane making a vertical take-off heading straight up toward heaven. Synchronistically, on the day he died she noticed in a newspaper a photo of a new type of plane that made vertical take-offs.

Christine's involvement in synchronistic events is not confined to precognitive dreams, as became evident in an incident related by Professor Bender.[3] In an attempt to see if Christine could dream "on demand," Bender gave her a key phrase that she was to meditate on before going to bed. The phrase was: "My lottery ticket wins the first prize." In the morning, Christine reported a dream that had nothing to do (apparently) with lotteries: "A street leading through a valley in the outskirts of Freiburg. Some villas. I had formerly been in one of them. A musician I know is living there. I recognize the house and ring the bell. A flaxen-haired young man wearing dark horn-rimmed spectacles answers when I ask for my acquaintance: 'No, he is not here,' and adds, 'He does not exist or it is not his house.' I am strangely bewildered by this contradiction and feel that something is wrong."

"The following evening," relates Bender, "Mrs. Mylius met an actress whom she had known when she lived in Freiburg some ten years ago. A collaborator at the Institute—an amateur actor who had proved to be a catalyst for paranormal events —had told her the day before that this actress had a young friend but his name was not given. Mrs. Mylius's colleague was accompanied by this friend: a flaxen-haired young man with dark-rimmed spectacles. It came out that he was the son of the musician Mrs. Mylius was trying to visit in her dream and that he lived in his father's house after his father's death some years ago. The key word 'dream' made the young man tell an extraordinary dream that he also had the night before: He had bought a lottery ticket and won 15,000 marks; enough to emigrate to Brazil where he wanted to escape from the police who were searching for him."

Attempting to separate the elements of this experience into categories like telepathy or precognition becomes cumbersome. When asked to dream about winning a lottery, Christine dreams about visiting a musician's house where only an unknown man with flaxen hair and horn-rimmed glasses lives. She meets this unknown man the next day, finds that he is the son of the musician friend, and that he had the lottery dream she was supposed to have had. The more economical explanation is synchronicity—a constellation of coincidences springing from a larger pattern or archetype in which several people are involved. Or, as Kurt Vonnegut might put it, this has the earmarks of a Kerass. Bender comments that "I find observations of this kind—if they are well documented—highly elucidating for an understanding of how psi works in life situations."

I had also noticed that dreams sometimes became a connecting link with future life situations. My first experience with this began on Saturday morning, February 5, 1966, when living in New York. I awoke with a dream fragment in mind, which I recorded: "Three pet hamsters or little furry creatures like them got loose. We went looking for them. I found one and carried him under my arm; the other two followed us home." As I was puzzling over what the dream could possibly mean, I got a collect telephone call from Reno, Nevada, from an army friend living in the West whom I had not seen for several years. He sounded drunk. He told me he had just gambled away seventy dollars, and wanted me to send him some money. I refused on the grounds that banks were not open on Saturday. He cursed me roundly and told me that he never wanted to see me again. I discounted that as he seemed very distressed. He had gotten drunk on Christmas Day, had an argument with his wife, kicked in the television set, and had left her and their small child.

This telephone call led me to venture an analysis of the dream to make a prediction: "Could the hamster-like creature symbolize a human being who has strayed—compare with Ron's call ten minutes later. Things are going to work out all right."

Ron came to New York a few weeks later and stayed with me while he was looking for work. I suggested he apply to a certain firm for work, which he did. He also applied to a box number advertisement for a job. It turned out that the box number was for the same firm that I had recommended. He got the job and worked in New York for a few months. Then, finally, he went to join his wife in another city. When I visited them five years later, I was struck by the pets he had brought the children: a pair of hamsters. Ron had completely given up drinking and now was finding a full life with his family and a successful business he and his wife had started. Indeed, things had worked out all right—by the time he had acquired some hamsters.

In April 1968, when in Freiburg, I began to record dreams regularly in an effort to see if any of them would eventually prove precognitive. A dream recorded on April 25 seemed a little bizarre:

> My wife and I were in a hotel room with a couple of other people, having something like a party. There was a little difficulty—the manageress said we had to leave by a certain hour, so we did. I spotted a building I felt was the Bollingen Foundation and entered the building. I was just in time for a lecture, which I found a little silly; it was given in German, English, and Dutch. The lady next to me had a conversation with me in German, complaining that she couldn't understand the speaker. I explained that he was then talking in Dutch. . . . I then returned to the hotel, and again we were told by what hour we must leave.

Two months before I had been in Utrecht, Holland, to visit the sensitive Gerard Croiset. During this time I had picked up a few Dutch words. On May 4 Croiset visited the Freiburg Institute to make some predictions for a "chair test" experiment in Zürich on May 6. This experiment, sponsored (surprisingly) by the Rosicrucians, was a type Croiset had often done before. Croiset would describe in detail a person who at a later date would be chosen by chance from a large audeince. Professor Bender and others from the Institute witnessed Croiset's predictions, which were tape recorded, and I was invited to go to Zürich on the test night of May 6 to verify any results.

I had never been in Zürich before so I first went to find the building where the experiment was to take place, and then my wife and I took a room in a small hotel nearby. The manageress lay great emphasis on the fact that the hotel closed its doors at midnight. At the lecture hall, a lecture written in

German by Croiset was read by someone else. And then Croiset started talking himself, repeating his predictions for the person who would be chosen by chance in a few minutes. Croiset's German was difficult to understand for the Swiss, especially since he kept throwing in Dutch words and even a few English words—such as *tape recorder* instead of *Tonbandgerät*. At one point a woman seated next to me on the stage asked me in German if I knew what a certain word was that Croiset had spoken. By sheer luck, I knew the word, which was Dutch, and I explained it to her. The chair test itself was successful, if a bit confused. Croiset hit a great many details of the life of a woman whose number came up and who came onto the stage. Then a man came on the stage to translate into proper German what Croiset was saying. Oddly enough, at this point Croiset's predictions shifted to describe this man. The Rosicrucians applauded the success of the experiment, and then a few of us went with Croiset to a nearby restaurant where we had a party. My wife and I had to leave early, however, in order to get back to our hotel by midnight—the hour set by the manageress.

The incorrect detail in the dream of the building being the Bollingen Foundation was partially due to my confusion between the Jung Institute in Zürich and the Bollingen Foundation in the United States, which sponsored Jungian studies. But certainly I have never before nor since attended a lecture in which Dutch, German, and English were confused.

It was during this time that I had the dreams about Robert Kennedy's assassination, described in Chapter 2. The most detailed dreams had come on May 25, 1968, but an earlier dream of May 19, 1968, led eventually four years later to an interpretation of the presidential death cycle. The dream was bizarrely ominous: "A man comes in with a bird following him. I say, 'Don't let that bird come near me! It's cursed.' He wondered how I knew, and I tell him about curses. . . . I had a parchment which was cursed, and around which things happened.

"Meanwhile, I got nervous about the bird, which is following me around the table. I get up on the table, and so does the bird, and I shoo it away.

"Also, I thought of Justine's stories of witchcraft, and also inserted was a story of Peleus. I can only recall a facemask with the letters made from pistols and weapons across it in black and red: P-e-l-e-u-s."

My associations to the dream were:

> The bird as carrying a curse would derive from my idea last night of the *imago*—an organizing image of the unconscious—from which a curse might proceed. The parchment reminds me of a film (*The Curse of the Demon*) in which a demon came when the appointed hour of a curse operated; the demon came to the man holding the parchment and killed him.
>
> Witchcraft makes use of magic—constructs an *imago* and invests it with strong emotional energy to carry out a curse. . . . Could the cycle of 20-year intervals actually be the result of a curse by an Indian chief on President Harrison? The idea seems appalling, but perhaps that curse fits into a larger pattern, and was originally even evoked by it.

The stories of witchcraft I referred to had been told me by an English writer, Justine Glass, who had written a book on witchcraft and, at the time I knew her in London, was writing a book on prophecy. When I last saw her in early 1968 before I left London, she told me that she had recently joined a witches' coven but had been cursed by the leader of another coven who had wanted her to coauthor a book with him. She had refused. The other witch committed suicide shortly afterward. Soon after, Justine's health had failed, and she confided to me she was worried about the curse. Members of the other witch's coven kept telephoning her and asking after her health. I learned much later that Justine died a very painful death in November 1968 from a liver ailment.

The name Peleus eluded me. I could not find any reference to it though I suspected it came from classical literature, which I had studied in college. But not until March 7, 1972, four years later, did I accidentally come upon a reference to Peleus in a book on Greek drama. I underlined a phrase in red: "A thoroughgoing melodramatist would have made great play with Peleus." Peleus had been a character in Euripides' *Medea*. Coincidentally, that same day I had drawn a sketch to depict the patterns of assassination. I used theatrical facemasks to represent the assassinated presidents and drew pistols to represent the assassins. Suddenly, I recalled the dream of May 19, 1968, and looked it up. There were all the elements of that strange passage: facemasks, pistols, and the name Peleus in black print and underlined in red.

This correspondence in itself was trivial, but it drew attention to the idea I had associated originally with the dream of a curse being the explanation for the twenty-year death cycle. The dream image of the accursed bird being shooed away now indicated to me that the presidential death cycle was over. Finally, after four years, I had been able to interpret the dream.

This type of correspondence of dream with future event is typical of a number of experiences. The apparently trivial precognized event (facemasks, pistols, and the name Peleus) carried with it a tremendous amount of emotion, both in the excitement I had that day in putting together finally a pattern of assassinations, and in the "Eureka!" feeling of finally finding out the meaning of that dream that literally had been haunting me. I would hazard the generalization that if one element of a dream (however apparently trivial) is precognitive, then the other elements of the dream, including its associations, will have some greater significance—either pointing to a future event or significance by itself. In other words, a partial fulfillment of a dream is like a finger pointing: "Here is something important."

By dint of a year's study of dreams, I was now improving in recognizing precognitive dreams beforehand and venturing predictions based on their analysis.

Interpretation of dream symbols must sometimes await future associations that explain them. Such was the case with a dream series that began on February 7, 1969, when I was living in Brooklyn and attempting to free-lance as an editor and writer. I had not yet published any writing. The dream was:

> I was working somewhere in an office. I felt I had to in-terview both Jeane Dixon and Ruth Montgomery that afternoon. I called up Jeane who very nicely said I could come over that afternoon for a reading. She lived on East 40th Street, and gave me directions for reaching her. . . . (At a bank) I picked up a sack of gold. . . .
>
> I was going to see Jeane not to investigate her, but for a reading on some writing I was doing. I was genuinely anxious to find out what was going to happen. I had decided not to see Ruth Montgomery after all that day since there just wasn't enough time. Jeane was very nice and gave me the reading without asking any questions of me; I believe it was favorable.

My analysis of it was: "Perhaps precognitive in a distorted way. Jeane Dixon lives in Washington, so perhaps she repre-sents someone else in life. The bag of gold suggests my com-ing into something valuable. . . . Perhaps this will happen in a period when I am working in an office. Last night Jeane Dixon's name came up in conversation."

About a week later I received a telephone call from Martin Ebon, the parapsychological writer and editor, who told me he might have some work for me eventually. He appeared in a dream of February 26: "I was in an office with Martin Ebon. He was sitting across at a desk. He had a very large, strange contraption which he said was a portable Xerox machine." My comment then was: "I talked with Ebon on the telephone about ten days ago or so. He said he would call me last week but didn't. The dream indicates he will call at some future time."

On March 11, Ebon did call me with a request that I write an article for a book on reincarnation that he was editing. The article was to be about the writer Joan Grant, who has published many novels that she says are remembered from previous lifetimes. By happy synchronicity, my neighbor downstairs had most of Joan Grant's novels, which she lent me for preparing the article. In addition, Ebon sent me some other material about her. I worked furiously over a weekend to write the article and finished it by March 17, a day that someone else had called me in to do some other work in an office. So it was indeed a "period when I am working in an office." From the office I telephoned Martin Ebon and told him I could bring him the article as I was anxious to know what he thought of it. I didn't know where his office was located, but he gave me directions: it was on East Fortieth Street. When I arrived, he was sitting at a desk and next to him was a portable photocopier, as in the dream. The association with Jeane Dixon became apparent as we discussed Jeane Dixon and Ruth Montgomery and he even showed me a picture of Jeane. Ebon's "reading" on my writing was favorable, and he gave me a check for it. He also commissioned me to do some more writing for him, thus starting me out on my writing career. The dream image of the "bag of gold" did seem appropriate.

The striking correspondence of the East Fortieth Street address was matched with another odd detail from a dream of December 29, 1968. In that dream "I was in a library. . . .

There was a stack of books, all the same title, on prophecy."
Ebon's office was lined with bookshelves, and prominent in
one corner was a stack of books, all the same title: *Prophecy
in Our Time*.

In a general way, too, the Jeane Dixon dream was prophetic
of my interviewing famous psychics for *Psychic* magazine
a couple of years later. *Psychic* magazine's first issue, which
appeared in June 1969, featured an interview by James Bolen
with Jeane Dixon, which is reprinted in the volume *Psychics*
(New York, Harper & Row, 1972), to which I wrote an introduction.

The most famous psychic I had known was Eileen Garrett,
to whom I felt indebted for starting me in parapsychology. I
often dreamed of her, though a dream of August 22, 1970,
seemed ominous: "I and another person were in the back of
a private airplane piloted by Eileen Garrett. She was giving
us a lift from some place. The door between the passengers
and her cockpit was open, and then we landed for a few minutes. She went out for a while. When she came back (which
I didn't see), a young man with a beard took over as pilot.
The other passenger and I knew that she was too ill to continue as pilot. The door to the cockpit was now closed."

I commented that the dream "seems very symbolic, and
suggestive of Eileen Garrett's 'piloting' of the Parapsychology
Foundation, which 'gave me a lift' once, i.e., a grant. This
might also be suggestive of her death, or her becoming even
more seriously ill than she is now. The closing of the cockpit
door suggests death. I'm not sure who the young man with
the beard might be. I mentioned Eileen Garrett last night in
my lecture, which may be the trigger for the dream."

That afternoon I fell asleep and recorded another dream
fragment: "I heard C's voice on the telephone telling me,
'Irene died yesterday from a heart attack.'" I commented in
my dream diary: "This morning I thought of Irene for a

moment. I had also, of course, been thinking about Eileen's death as predicted in the earlier dream. . . . It may be though that Irene is a substitution for someone else. Eileen, perhaps?"

That same afternoon, at 3:35 PM, as reported the next day in *The New York Times*, a pilot flying a Boeing 707 had a heart attack while making his approach to land at Kennedy Airport. His copilot took the controls and brought the plane safely in. I wonder now if the copilot had a beard.

Less than a month later, on September 15, 1970, Eileen Garrett died of a heart attack in the South of France. She had been seriously ill but had courageously staved off death until the completion of her international conference. I first heard the news when C telephoned me.

The ways in which a dream can relate to several connected events in the future can be demonstrated by an exotic dream I had on March 30, 1970: "I found an intriguing looking package. It was long and round, and had a label: 'A genuine Egyptian mummy's arm.' Then I was startled to see a little window in it. From the window came a snake's head, which frightened me. As the snake emerged, I saw that it was really a flying serpent—actually a large goose with a snake's neck and head. It flew toward me. I was both frightened and fascinated at having discovered the ancient fabled flying serpent."

My comments were: "An association is from a movie I saw years ago in which there was a flying serpent, supposed to be the legendary Quetzalcoatl, the god of the Aztecs. . . . It's interesting that I should confuse the Aztec and Egyptian cultures. Perhaps that indicates my coming across some connection between them that relates to some common cultural theme."

A few days later, on April 3, I was invited to visit an Egyptian friend I had not seen in many years. He introduced me to a friend who had lived in South America with a native tribe. I noticed on the wall a curious piece of wood fashioned in the shape of a goose's neck and head. That night, after I left them, I stopped in a bar and was both frightened and fascinated by a three-foot-long snake that a girl next to me was handling. I seemed to have combined the goose's head and the snake in my dream because I would see them a few hours apart.

Then, on April 11, I again visited the young man from South America who showed me some ancient mummy wrappings he had discovered and asked me to give a psychic reading on them. I described a nearby temple that held a statue of a South American god that was half-beast and half-man, like the Egyptian Sphinx. He said that such a temple had been near the place where he found the mummy. Thus the events of the following days mirrored the exotic elements of the dream: Egyptian, mummy, goose, snake, and South American god.

My initial conclusion from the dream, that there is a common cultural connection between the Aztecs and the Egyptians, is now supported by one of America's foremost archaeological scholars, Cyrus H. Gordon, in his book *Before Columbus* (London: Turnstone, 1972). His chapter on "The Plumed Serpent" shows the common traditions of the Egyptians and South Americans of a serpent god and reminds us of the Aztec tradition that "the arts of civilization were brought to America by a bearded white personage named Quetzalcoatl, 'The Plumed Serpent.' He came from the east by boat, which can only mean across the Atlantic."

Sometimes dreams can be very helpful, even profitable, if they are paid attention to. In a dream I had October 23, 1969, I was trying to brush off a persistent book salesman. "When I looked at one book, I was delighted, however. It dated from the 1880s, and the covers were coming off. It was very thick and part of it seemed to be a directory of some sort, listing names. It was a rare book on psychic phenomena, but man man selling it wanted too much: $30.00. I was trying to get his price down." I commented that "this may be partially precognitive of my coming across an old, valuable book in psychical research."

The very next day I was invited to visit a friend's apartment that I had never been to before. Many books lined the walls. Recalling my dream, I decided to browse among the books to see if any matched the dream description. I discovered a thick, century-old book that had a chapter on clairvoyants in New York. There was also a directory-like part that listed women's belongings of that period. I copied out the chapter on clairvoyants and sold it to *Psychic* magazine for somewhat more than the $30.00 of my dream. Happily, instead of paying out the money I was receiving it.

A common experience that baffles psychologists is the feeling people sometimes have of experiencing something as if for the second time. Called *déjà vu* ("already seen"), this experience seems to me to be often caused by forgotten precognitive dreams. I very nearly had such an experience one morning (December 27, 1968) when I awoke without recalling any dreams. A couple of hours later I looked out the window and saw the postman coming. Then, suddenly, I recalled a dream and ran to my typewriter: "A series of postcards about psychic things in England. They were all linked together, which was confusing until I realized that M had sent them." M is a friend in England who is active in psychic matters. I had not heard from her for many months.

By the time I had typed out my dream, the postman had arrived. In the mail were several Christmas cards and one postcard from England from M, which mentioned the College of Psychic Studies. My dream seemed to have linked together the other cards with the psychic postcard from England. Very likely, if I had not remembered that dream, I might have been wondering why I was getting a feeling of déjà vu.

The awesome powers of the unconscious mind were symbolized to me once in a dream that had a moral:

> I was in a cave, swimming about in a shallow pool when a powerful Tarzan-like man appeared with a tiger. I was very frightened of the tiger, but I tried not to let on. The man was bragging a bit about the prowess of his tiger and how well trained it was. He pointed out a large pool outside the cave but very far down the mountain side. He said he would order his tiger to dive into that distant pool and return. That seemed to be an incredible feat but the tiger did it. When the tiger returned it had to pass over me, which frightened me even more. But I worked up courage and said, "That was very good." I was astonished when the tiger replied, "Thank you." "My God," I thought, "it can speak English." And I was no longer afraid of the tiger, but admired it the more.

The dream symbolically states that if one learns to communicate with the psychic levels in the unconscious that psi needs no longer to be feared. Indeed, it is capable of extraordinary feats if trained—it can dive into the distant pool of the unconscious yet in the future and bring it back to consciousness. I had that dream on December 19, 1967, shortly before I began to explore seriously the prophetic potential of dreams. My five-year journey through dreams has taught me much, not only about prophecy, but also about myself. For to analyze dreams for possible precognitive content, one must first learn to analyze them for symbols in relation to past and present experience. Building up a personal dream-symbol dictionary enables one to recognize the symbolic significance of real-life events and their continuity from past through the present into the future.

The dream, triggered by a recent event that has emotional significance, expresses the event in symbols that are derived from similar events in both the past and the future. Could it be, I wonder, that the symbols, as archetypes, come first? That the events of our lives preexist as symbolic archetypes that are then expressed both in dreams and in real-life situations? That both our dreams and our lives are an enactment of archetypes of the unconscious? The meaningful coincidences or synchronicities linking the dreams and real-life events suggest this may be so—that both derive from a common origin in the archetypes of the timeless unconscious. For archetypes whose role in real life remains in the future, the dream may be a key to self-prophecy.

How do you tell a precognitive dream from its lesser brethren? The first step is to ask yourself if it makes sense in terms of past experience. Is it a jumble of past events? Then it's probably an ordinary dream. Or are there some elements that don't make sense, things that have never happened, people you have never met, situations that you have never encountered? These are pointers to precognition, especially if there is an accompanying emotion that seems to be greater than the dream scene implies. If you attempt to analyze *all* your dreams, then you should quickly develop an ability to place them in time and to pinpoint their relevance to your present situation. It is written in the Talmud that not analyzing a dream is like throwing away a letter unopened. (Of course dreams, like the mail, contain a lot of junk, too.)

I wish I could report that now I have become infallible in recognizing precognitive dreams. But alas, they slip by me, too. Generally, because they are so fantastic that I think nothing like that could possibly happen. But it does, though with the usual dream condensation and distortion. For instance, recently I awakened with a dream so odd and with such a terrifying emotion that I wrote it down just to dispel it. I was getting an injection to make me a teen-ager again. But I was afraid of the needle (it was a long needle, which they

were going to insert in my gums) since I had no memory
of the last time they had made me a teen-ager. Apparently
the injection also wiped out memory traces. The man with
the needle came toward me, and I awoke.

A few hours later someone told me about a man who had
become a teen-ager again through Primal Therapy, and he was
stuck there. He had all the attitudes of a teen-ager and enjoyed
them, thereby avoiding his responsibilities as an adult. That
afternoon a man told me he had "enjoyed several hours at the
dentist." Astonished at his attitude, I found out that he was
able to lower his pain threshold, often to the irritation of the
dentist. He told me he would do anything to avoid having a
long needle put in his gums. And he went into a dramatic re-
telling of a traumatic experience of this once happening. So,
within a few hours, the unlikely elements of the dream happened, and I had not suspected precognition.

The web of time through which dreams and events seem to
be interrelated in underlying patterns makes me suspect that,
in some ways, life is a dream. By that I mean that the elements
of real-life situations also can be analyzed and broken down
into symbols in the same way as dreams and that they can have
the same emotional significance (as well as paranormal significance). This, of course, would be akin to divination—but
would not be limited to special ceremonies or practices; it is
the observance of relationships and symbols (as well as their
associations) in a present situation that might have implications
for the future. This is what I have been calling synchronistic
patterns. Analyzing these patterns would seem to be more of
an art than a science, much like analyzing dreams.

In some odd ways, the events even *behave* like dreams. It is,
for example, a psychoanalytic premise that thoughts suppressed
during the day tend to emerge at night for full expression in
the dream. Take as a hypothetical example this case: A man
looks out of his office window and sees a man walking his

Peruvian llama. The girls in the office excitedly point at it. The man remembers a bawdy remark, about syphilis originating from human sexual contact with the llama, but suppresses it. That night he dreams that he sees a man walking a llama, and a woman walking beside him. "Didn't you know," she says, "they passed a law that makes it illegal for a man to walk a llama without a woman present."

The suppressed thought becomes transformed in the dream in our hypothetical case. Actually, though, the case is *not* hypothetical; yet there is a falsification. There *was* a man walking his llama. The man in the office (me) *did* suppress the bawdy remark to the ladies. But instead of a dream, I was handed a book a few minutes later—a review copy freshly arrived from the publisher—and opened it to a page in which the reasons were given for Peru having a law that made it illegal for a man to herd llamas without the presence of a woman.

I still have no explanation for *why* there was a man walking his llama near our office window, but one possible reason for the synchronistic effect of the book was that I had been in correspondence with parapsychologist Dr. Jule Eisenbud for some time trying to gain his interest in the concept of ("that Jungian heresy") synchronicity. The next day, at a parapsychological symposium at the University of California at Berkeley I listened to a talk by Dr. Eisenbud on psi and psychoanalysis and then told him my anecdote to bolster my cause. He was interested until he realized it didn't have anything to do with a real dream. A few minutes later I was walking along in a street in Berkeley telling a friend about the llama incident when I looked up and saw over a shop a large painted sign of a Peruvian llama.

The synchronistic effect of the three llamas did not seem to point to any future event, but it did make me focus on the idea that the cases described by Dr. Eisenbud in his fascinating book *Psi and Psychoanalysis* (Grune & Stratton, 1970) show evidence of the same phenomena that I have been describing: a complex interweaving of events and paranormal dreams that could easily have fit into my chapter on the Clockwork Kerass. Being a Freudian, Dr. Eisenbud is mistrustful of Jungian concepts such as synchronicity. His main objection, however, I share: the notion of *acausality*. In his essay "Why Psi?" in the *Psychoanalytic Review* (Winter 1966-7), Eisenbud argues convincingly that psi is the underlying force in human and even animal interrelationships and that instincts (can they be any different from primordial archetypal patterns?) overpower rational action.

Dr. Eisenbud has just finished his magnum opus on precognitive dreams in the psychoanalytic situation, which may well provide corroborative evidence that the patterns of human life are woven together in an incredibly complex web whose design preexists—and therefore can be precognized. Defining the identity of this Architect is a problem I shall leave to theologians.

8

A Psychic Tear in Time

The dreams we record in our dream diaries some time after wakening often are tidied up by our logical mind to make sense—details are altered or forgotten; new endings may be added or new beginnings are imagined to make the story come out right. The closest that modern science can come to revealing the "true" dream is in the dream laboratory. An electroencephalograph detects the characteristic brainwave patterns of dreaming and the accompanying rapid eye movements (REM). The dreamer can then be awakened to report his dream in full.

The Maimonides Dream Laboratory in Brooklyn, which has been investigating ESP dreams for ten years, conducted two experimental series in precognitive dreaming with the English sensitive Malcolm Bessent. In both series, Bessent was successful in dreaming about events he was to witness the next day. The statistical odds against this precognitive success were 5,000 to 1 in the first series and 1,000 to 1 in the second series. The judging system and results are described in *Dream Telepathy*, by M. Ullman and S. Krippner, with A. Vaughan (Macmillan, 1973).

A surprising finding in the second Bessent series was that slide programs shown before he went to sleep had less impact on his dreams than slide programs shown the next day. In other words, his dreams showed more effects from the future than from the past. Beginning in 1973, the Maimonides Dream Laboratory is undertaking an experimental study with a grant from the National Institute for Mental Health to investigate the difference between the effect on dreams of telepathic targets and targets viewed before going to bed.

A strong factor affecting dreams is, of course, motivation. If a person attempts to dream telepathically or precognitively, then he is much more likely to do so. It also helps if he believes it is possible. This may explain why ESP dreams occur at the Maimonides Dream Laboratory far more often than in ordinary life (as far as we know). In an eight-night dream-telepathy series in which I participated as a subject in the spring of 1969, I tried also to dream precognitively. I summarized one interesting experience in a letter to the *Journal of the American Society for Psychical Research* (January 1971, pp. 118-122):

> In the spring of 1969 I was a subject for an eight-night dream-telepathy series in the Maimonides Dream Laboratory, Brooklyn. The experimenters were Dr. Stanley Krippner and Mr. Charles Honorton. Dr. Krippner urged me also to look for precognition in my dreams, and I found several dreams that seemed to be precognitive of events occurring in my life a day or so afterward. The dream series was completed in April, though I did not get the official transcripts until some time later.
>
> In mid-July, 1969, I met with Dr. Montague Ullman, Director of the Maimonides Mental Health Center, which includes the Dream Laboratory, and discussed with him an article I was writing on the Lab for *Psychic*. We also talked briefly about precognitive dreaming, and I promised to send him some examples from my own records. I then read through the transcripts of the dream-telepathy series to see if there might be additional precognitive dreams. In a letter to Dr. Ullman dated July 17, 1969, I pointed out a dream of April 3, 1969, as being possibly precognitive of a

future experiment at the Lab. The following are excerpts from the post-sleep interview:

"*Fifth Dream Report:* Chuck [Honorton] was looking over a report of some previous experiment, and he had marked for some reason through the transcript 'Fs' which meant failures. . . . There was a television set in the room . . . as I was looking at it, I watched a scene. There was a man with a knife in his hand and out in a corner was outstretched a monkey, sort of lying there. . . .
"*Post-sleep Interview:* I was lying in bed and Chuck Honorton was there and he was marking a transcript and he was using the letter 'F' as a symbol for something. . . . He said, 'Oh, "F" is for failure.' . . . Then I looked at the television set there and this television set actually seemed to be part of the experiment as well . . . as I looked at it, the whole thing began to move and come to life, and there was a man holding a knife . . . and behind him was a monkey lying on the floor, and there may have been someone else there as well. . . . I wonder if there might be sometime an experimental thing like this. . . ."

On January 12, 1970, the Canadian television personality Norman Perry arrived at the Dream Laboratory to film an experiment for Canadian TV. Perry was to be the dream subject, and I was to be a back-up subject in case he couldn't get to sleep. A target pool of pictures had been made up the day before, and that night the agent, Don Rice, was in another building looking at the randomly selected target pictures. Charles Honorton was the experimenter.

In the morning, after Perry's and my dreams were recorded, the target pool was brought in and we made our judgings from the experimenter's notes. I judged a miss. It turned out that my dreams were only about the agent's associations with the target, and not about the target itself. Perry, however, scored a direct hit. And since I was there only as a back-up subject, it was decided to film Perry's judgings alone. As the cameras for the TV show went into action, I watched the scene. Several other persons watched as well. Perry put the oversized target pictures on the floor and pointed out his first choice: a photo of an albino monkey. This corresponded with his dream image of a white animal and the strikingly correct detail of a blue broadloom rug. Perry then pointed out his second choice: a man holding an axe.

These, then, are the correspondences between my dream and the actual events: (*a*) I was lying in bed (as a subject for a dream experiment). (*b*) Charles Honorton was there. (*c*) A transcript from a previous experiment (that of April 3rd) was pertinent. (*d*) My judging was a failure. (*e*) I watched the scene. (*f*) Instead of a television set, there were cameras for television. (*g*) There was a "monkey" lying on the floor. (*h*) Instead of a man holding a knife, there was a man holding an axe. (*i*) There were other people present. (*j*) It was "an experimental thing."

It may be that the unusual excitement of a television filming singled out in my unconscious that particular experiment to dream about nine months before it took place. Moreover, I have for several years been attempting to document precognition in an irrefutable way. Thus, a unique opportunity was offered not only to record on tape the dream itself, but also to film its fulfillment.

One reason for singling out that dream as precognitive of a future experiment at the Dream Lab was, of course, that the setting was the Dream Laboratory. Another was the appearance of a television set. At that time I did not own a television set nor had I recently watched anything on someone else's set. The dream precognitively focused on an event of more than usual interest, since during the course of the experiment I chatted with Norman Perry about precognitive dreams and the Central Premonitions Registry. Perry then invited me to appear on his nationwide television show in Canada, "Perry's Probe," the following October. After the taping of our conversation about precognitive dreams, especially those I had of Robert Kennedy's assassination, I stayed on in the studio to watch the taping of another segment with the author of a new book. The author was Jeanne Gardner, and her book

(*A Grain of Mustard*) told of a premonition she had experienced of Robert Kennedy's assassination. Synchronicity once again seemed to be afoot.

On April 18, 1969, the last night of the dream-telepathy experiment, I came to the Dream Lab with two dreams I had had that morning. I told them to the experimenters:

> Two dreams I had early this morning at home might conceivably have something to do with the target [picture] tonight. In the dream I was at a university and it was the last day of the term and I got a call from Dr. Krippner. He told me that I had missed several chemistry lab sessions but that he would let me make it up today. I said that was very kind of him and yes indeed I would come over to the lab. . . . I pulled out what appeared to be a college catalogue trying to figure out what time the lab was open, but all I could find in the catalogue were pictures. I looked at these various pictures and I was somewhat confused. Then the scene rapidly changed to a different dream in which a young woman I know was pictured. She was standing there with a friend and was complaining about a horse. . . . I saw this girl in a play a couple of weeks ago in which she was singing a song about "He is my thing," and the "thing" was a monster as portrayed by a nude man wearing rather hideous looking accouterments, but it might be possible that the target picture for tonight might somehow fit in with this theme.

It was not until nearly two years later, on February 20, 1972, that I learned which telepathic target picture my agent had been looking at during that session. I talked with Dr. Krippner, who told me I could come to the Lab to look over the pictures, which he would identify. We went through the dream transcripts, and Dr. Krippner marked each segment as to which target picture the agent had been looking at so we could write this up as a chapter in *Dream Telepathy*. The best telepathic hit for that April 18 session was an untitled picture by the British artist Francis Bacon. It shows a gruesome-looking monster who is black and who holds a black umbrella. Around him are carcasses of meat. The background is purple and has dark purple panels in diamond shapes. Thus I learned that my dreams the morning of April 18 were precognitive of looking over the pictures at the lab and especially at the one of the monster.

The dream I had on April 18 *while* the agent was looking at the monster picture was long and involved:

> I recall . . . being at, I think, not an actor's house, but perhaps a studio, because it was as if something were being filmed, and the actor was wearing either a mask or most intensive makeup, like Boris Karloff used to do in his Frankenstein movies, and in the story he was attacking someone else, and I told him . . . "Oh, don't you recall? I did a [psychic] reading for you in which I said you'd be acting like a monster and I didn't realize it would be a literal sort of thing." And he just glowered at me. . . . I couldn't tell really if that was the effect of the makeup. . . .
>
> One person I met . . . knitted sweaters that had seams on them, and he was wearing basically a purple sweater and I think he may have been Negro. . . . [The sweater] had a very elaborate scene on it, sort of in a diamond shape. . . . He showed me the label and I think the label said "Anderson." And he said, "No, I make these. These are sold at Gimbels at their outlet on 23rd Street. . . ."

With the dream fresh in mind, I went that evening to see a play that a friend was appearing in. Before the play began I was introduced to someone who told me he knew Dr. Krippner and had attended his wedding. This started the synchronistic feel of the evening. Attending the play with me was a friend, an actor, whom I had given a psychic reading for a few days before. I had told him that one day he would play a Frankenstein-type monster role. In the play we saw the lead actor was a Negro playing a man named Anderson. My actor friend in the play was also a Negro and wore intensive facial makeup and a sweater he had made himself: it had large diamond shapes sewn on it. He was wearing purple trousers. After the play, I met another actor friend who told me that he was no longer acting. "What are you doing now?" I asked. He opened his coat to show me his wool knit shirt. "I make these and sell them uptown at a boutique." Later, I went to a party at the apartment of still another actor and found all the people I had met earlier in attendance.

So, while the dream of April 18, 1969, was triggered telepathically by a target painting of a monster with purple diamond shapes in the background, the most detailed correspondences of the dream came on the day I finally saw the picture, twenty-two months later. Especially striking are the name Anderson and the sweaters being made for a store. My dream seems to have condensed the various actors I met that night into one. The link with a play seems to go back to the second part of my dream on the morning of April 18, 1969, about a play with a monster.

A clue that my nocturnal monster dream related to the future was provided by a segment of the dream that specified that "it was as though I were suddenly thrown into the future and from the future was trying to precognize something still farther in the future." That portion of the dream, cited in an earlier chapter, I had copied out and sent to the Central Premonitions Registry as possibly precognitive of a newspaper article on the CPR. That part of the dream also was fulfilled in 1972.

Both the monkey dream and the monster dream offer excellent evidence for precognition since they were recorded a few minutes after occurring in the laboratory. Both of them contained numerous specific details of a future situation, thus presumably ruling out fulfillment by chance coincidence. But, as also in the dreams that I recorded at home, these dreams contained wrong details as well. And, as usual in dreams of all sorts, they were characterized by symbolic distortions.

Contrast these dreams with the cases reported to psychical researchers *after* the fulfilled event. Such cases usually bear the tag line: "The dream was fulfilled in every detail." It would seem, however, that this is not true—rather the mind "corrects" the dream retrospectively to make it fit more exactly the situation. The same sort of retrospective correction crops up in other previsionary experiences and can often mislead theorizers of time. For instance, in J. B. Priestley's handsome volume *Man and Time* (New York: Doubleday, 1964), the celebrated case of Sir Victor Goddard's prevision of the Drem Airfield in Scotland is cited (p. 229): "While flying in mist and rain over Scotland in 1934, Goddard saw what should have been Drem Airfield below him. But instead of the disused hangars among fields that Drem was at the time, the airfield appeared to be in full working order, with blue-overalled mechanics among four yellow aircraft. Four years later, the details of Goddard's experience were exactly fulfilled: The airport was rebuilt, training aircraft were then painted yellow (instead of silver, as formerly), and blue overalls had become standard wear for flight mechanics."

Now, if that were actually true, it might suggest that precognition is literally a "time trip" into the future, à la H. G. Wells's *The Time Machine*. The truth of the matter is that Goddard based his account of the airfield's changes on what a friend had told him. When many years later Goddard actually visited the airfield, he discovered that the hangars were not remodeled as he had seen them; instead, the old hangars had been knocked down and new ones of entirely different design and made with different materials had been erected. Goddard published this new light on his interesting experience in 1966.[1]

The tendency to correct prophetic dreams or experiences

retrospectively does not reflect negatively on a person's character, but rather is a fundamental quality of perception. We tend to see things in patterns and shapes. Our senses apprehend a partial gestalt, or pattern, and register it as the whole or perfect form. For centuries astronomers pictured the paths of the planets as perfect circles instead of the ellipses they actually are. The fisherman who tells about the "one that got away" is not necessarily lying, but may actually be remembering falsely, his memory influenced by what "should have been."

In dreams, distortion is the rule, whether about past or future events. The British sensitive Jane Sherwood cites a humorous example of her daughter's reaction to the fulfillment of a prophetic dream:

> My little daughter, aged six, was joyfully anticipating her birthday. No doubt her mind was full of the possibility of parcels containing toys, dolls and sweets, the natural kind of birthday present which the postman might be expected to bring on the happy morning. Two nights before her birthday she dreamed that she had a parcel from her grandmother and that when she opened it there were two lovely birds inside. She was delighted with her dream and insisted on telling us every detail. . . .
>
> I listened to the rambling recital of this dream over the breakfast table, and not being particularly interested in the subject of dreams at that time should have thought no more about it but for the sequel. For the great morning came, the postman staggered up with a load of parcels and among them was a box-shaped package from her grandmother in the country. My daughter had apparently forgotten her dream and began speculating on its contents: a doll? No, parcel too short for that; a game? No, it didn't rattle; and finally, "I expect it's only clothes," she said with resignation. But the wrappings disclosed a plump partridge and a note explaining that as she had been ill, her granny thought this would help to make her better. It was a joint present from her

granny and her uncle, for the latter had shot it and she had dressed it. The child considered it in silence and then said, "It ought to have been two." Then she turned to other matters and made no more reference to her dream. Two birds in the dream; it was of course *two gifts* in one, and this being too subtle a thing for the child-mind to record had been symbolized in the dream as *two birds*.[2]

This type of symbolization is scarcely unique to children; for in dreams we all become as little children: symbols are the language of the unconscious.

The concepts of the *eternal now* and the *timeless unconscious* occur regularly in the writings of mystics, whether they be psychics, such as Edgar Cayce, or psychologists, such as Jung. Spiritualistic writings frequently refer to "another dimension" in which discarnate entities exist. Psychic sensitives often describe a feeling of being "outside of time" when they are receiving psychic impressions. A very similar state is often described by users of psychedelic drugs. Could this experience be a subjective hallucination? Many psychologists think so.

Yet, from an entirely different quarter, there emerges well-attested (if rare) evidence that another dimension does exist. Prof. Hans Bender has reported on a number of poltergeist investigations in Germany in which matter passed through matter: that is, *teleportation*. Witnesses actually observed, for instance, the teleportation of nails from a basement cupboard to a few inches below the ceiling upstairs, where, forming in the air, the nails became visible and fell to the floor. A bottle put on a kitchen table materialized outside a house at the level of the roof and fell to earth in a zigzag path. Professor Bender's coat disappeared from a closet to be found lain neatly on the snow outside the house. There were no footprints. To one of Germany's most eminent physicists, Ernst Mach, genuine disappearance and reappearance of objects would offer the best evidence for the reality of a fourth dimension, a higher or "other" space that allows for a four-fold freedom of movement. Although the concept of such a fourth dimension has been around since at least the 1880s, no one has yet been able to experimentally demonstrate its reality.

Apports (teleportation of small objects) are traditionally said to occur in the presence of physical mediums, much in the same way as the teleportation phenomena occur in the presence of poltergeist children. Could there be some connection between this physical (psychokinetic) activity and that of mental psi? When one poltergeist boy was tested by Bender with ESP cards, the boy guessed all twenty-five correctly. Bender ran him through three more times, and three more times the boy guessed all twenty-five correctly. In fact, the boy may have established a world record for correct ESP card guesses. When Bender tested a poltergeist girl for ESP, she too scored well above chance—but only when emotionally aroused, such as when the psychokinetic incidents tended to occur.

Other testimony that psychics can penetrate another dimension comes from Dr. Andrija Puharich, who says that out of twenty attempts by the Israeli psychic Uri Geller to dematerialize objects 75 percent were successful and of attempts to rematerialize them 60 percent were successful. Puharich postulates other dimensional existence for the missing three objects.[3] Geller has demonstrated mental ESP against odds of a trillion to one. This link between physical and mental psi phenomena indicates to me that a sensitive's psi field may be capable of penetration into another dimension—one in which space and time, as we conventionally know them, have no dominion.

In late 1971 I interviewed Dr. Gertrude Schmeidler, one of America's foremost parapsychologists, for *Psychic* magazine.

I was fascinated to discover that she had not only played around with the idea of another dimension but had even thought of a way to test the hypothesis: "We can think of ESP or PK as making a fold in the universe and producing contact between two things ordinarily separated, but doing this without making any upset in the everyday set of relationships." She theorized that if a person makes contact through ESP with a distant target, he may, as it were, be creating a "fold" in the universe. Once he has made this fold, it could perhaps be used by others. If the target is a complex one, and both persons describe the same details, the explanation could be telepathy between them; but if they describe different details, it implies that they were making independent contact with the target material, with one person using the fold made by the other person.

Some months later, in March 1972, I once again thought of Dr. Schmeidler's hypothesis as a way of explaining some odd correspondences I found when describing the patterns of dream-target correspondences in a dream-telepathy experiment in which I had been one of two subjects. In this experiment, part of the so-called Vaughan study done by the Maimonides Dream Laboratory, a telepathic agent in a distant room concentrated on the same picture for four nights while Robert Harris, at the time a fourteen-year-old high-school student, slept in one monitored sleep room and I slept in another such room a few yards away. Both Harris and I expected a different target picture to be used for each of those four nights (half the study), but we did not find out the experiment's design until after we judged our dreams for correspondence with a target pool of pictures later. Although the study was judged only for telepathic correspondences with the target pictures, I was attempting to dream also about future targets—that is, precognitively.

For these four nights, my dreams bore no resemblance to

the target picture the agent was looking at. Yet the dream transcripts bore unusually great correspondences with pictures that had been left in their sealed envelopes and which I saw, finally, on April 21, 1969. The most striking of these apparently precognitive correspondences was an image on February 14 about three comedians named Lilly, Lolly, and Louie who lived in bird houses to a target picture entitled *Lilly and the Sparrows.*

My transcript of February 21 had great correspondence with a target picture *Washington and Lafayette at the Battle of Yorktown.* Washington and Lafayette are shown on horseback surveying rows of infantry battling on a grassy meadow. Three of the soldiers have just been hit by bombshells. On the right are a row of mounted cavalry.

Some imagery that corresponded with this target was: "An out-of-doors scene. I seemed to sense animals . . . in a field . . . like an ox or horse." An imaginary song, "Let Us Lead the Life of Leisure, Lazarus," seemed to hint at Lafayette, since my association was: "The word *Lazaret* refers to France. I mean, it's a French word for hospital for the wounded, usually during war time."

In other imagery, "I seemed to be in a large grounds, grassy grounds and there seemed to be a hospital. . . . Men there were wounded. . . . They were all dressed alike; some sort of hospital clothing, and I was helping to heal them. I went to one who had something wrong with his jaw . . . and another person had something else wrong. . . . It's odd that such a dream should be located out of doors." I added later, "They seemed to be veterans who I felt had somehow been wounded during war."

Meanwhile, the same night, Robert Harris was dreaming of "a sort of a farm and it was during the war . . . World War II . . . and there was this dog . . . a real hero dog . . . and it went around saving people's lives." The dominant colors of this dream were brown and white, the colors of the two horses in the picture. In a later dream, "It was like there was a war going on . . . and they were placing the injured there . . . they were taking people into the army. . . . Like when the guy would come around and say, 'Oh, we have someone new with a fractured leg here, move over a little bit.' "

In the morning, I guessed the target "might be a picture painted during the war. . . . I think it's likely that it will be out of doors."

Harris guessed that "it probably would be something about war because most of my dreams had war in them."

So we both incorporated elements of the picture into our dreams: both of us saw wounded soldiers; I was hinting at the name Lafayette; Harris described the colors of the horses.

My transcript of February 28 showed great correspondence with a picture entitled *The Engineer Heartfield*, by George Grosz. A sinister-looking German engineer with a green head and a blue and gray torso is shown in a three-quarters view. Little wheels and machinery take the place of his heart. Like a cartoon cutout, he stands in a large room with massive stone walls of gray-brown.

Corresponding imagery began with "something vaguely sinister about it . . . and there was also an odd little scene, almost like a cartoon . . . and then . . . a scene which seemed to be carved out of great natural hewn blocks of granite." The little wheels of the picture seemed to correspond with an image of shooting at targets. "They have wheels with ducks or birds . . . and you try your luck with a rifle."

In later imagery, I had been "transformed into a German doctor . . . and I speak with a heavy German accent, asking directions how to get to the lab." Later I saw a photographer: "There was something kind of disgusting about this man. . . . But he went into this large room to photograph, and someone said, 'Oh, he stood three-quarters back.' " This corresponds with the three-quarters view of the German engineer.

My guess about the target was: "I don't think it was a very pretty sort of picture at all. I think it might be sort of sinister."

Meanwhile that night Harris was dreaming that "the kids . . . got their height checked, then the guy wrote it down and then put it in the computer." The colors were brown and gray. In a later dream, "there was this guy who my sister got to know and he was going to die . . . and also we had a chameleon in our refrigerator, and it was really a distinct color—green against red." In a later dream, he saw gray and brown again, and said, "I get an eerie feeling about the whole thing." Machinery appeared again in his sixth dream: "There was an EEG there, and everybody was sticking their fingers into it." In his last dream, "I was just standing up and they were on their knees worshipping . . . and they were really getting mad at me—they almost like practically killed me. . . . There was a lot of green."

Harris's guess about the target was: "Something that would have a lot of brown and green and . . . people. There could be something with a doctor . . . a doctor being there operating the machine."

Harris's dream correspondences with that target included the colors, the doctor (when compared with my German doctor), the computer, and other machinery. My dream correspondences included the granite room, the three-quarters view, the German doctor, but not the colors, nor the other machinery beside the wheels.

An odd thing about those nights was that the imagery I have quoted here from my transcripts was taken exclusively from non-REM imagery—that is, imagery seen in meditation and other altered states that are not dreams. Harris's imagery, on the other hand, comes only from dreams. I had at that time been experimenting with getting ESP impressions during meditation and was curious to find out if meditation might be a better way of getting ESP impressions than dreams. During meditation I often feel an enlargement of my psychic field—that is, as if I somehow extend beyond the confines of my body. Such an experience has been called *field consciousness* by the parapsychologist W. G. Roll, who is project director for the Psychical Research Foundation in Durham, North Carolina. Many mystics and sages have reported that ESP incidents sometimes arise during these meditative periods of field consciousness.

What may have been happening, then, on those nights that Harris and I were in nearby sleep rooms was that I expanded my psychic field during meditation to tune in to the distant (in space or time) target pictures and influenced him to dream about the same pictures I was tuning in to. The fact that he got several details of the pictures that I did not tends to support Dr. Schmeidler's hypothesis that a sensitive makes a fold in the universe—a psychic tear in space-time—through another dimension. And that another person can make use of this psychic tear once it is formed by a sensitive.

Once before, I had been intrigued with hypothetical ideas put forward by Dr. Schmeidler. In her presidential address to the Parapsychological Association Convention in Durham, North Carolina, on September 10, 1971, Dr. Schmeidler noted that many parapsychologists were coming to believe that ESP and PK could not easily be separated. Perhaps they were part of a unitary process? That evening I discussed the idea with one of her doctoral students at City College of New York, Larry Lewis, who had found in his experiments an odd, inexplicable relationship between subjects' alpha brainwaves and the automatic recording of lights by a so-called Schmidt machine.

The next morning I recorded a dream that put great emphasis on Lewis and the puzzle of psi: "I was in a competition with a group to put together a gigantic puzzle. I was very quick. It was like an enormous geographic entity, and I added the last few elements when I got the clue 'twelve toes' which looked like two six-toed feet facing each other. They represented Manhattan, with the Statue of Liberty at the very end, sitting on its pedestal that looked like a star-shaped wall.

"It seemed to be an organization. The head woman was going to take me to see someone since this excellence was unusual. . . . The last part of the dream was taking a bus with a friend. . . . I thought of Larry Lewis." The middle part of the dream had to do with a bottle of "immortality" pills. On waking, I thought of the puzzle solving as finding the unitary process of ESP and PK. The Statue of Liberty is an ESP target picture I sometimes use with groups. The bottle suggested a friend's experience of psychokinetically moving a small bottle by "zapping" it: it had moved a few inches in one direction, then a few inches in another direction. My interpretation of the dream was: "The puzzle of psi. The woman leader is Gertrude Schmeidler."

A few months later, on December 28, 1971, I again attended a Parapsychological Association function—the PA's symposium in Philadelphia for the annual convention of the American Association for the Advancement of Science. Larry Lewis read a paper entitled "EEG-Alpha Relations with Non-Intentional and Purposeful ESP." It contained a graphed relationship between a blue light (one of four lights) and a subject's alpha level. Rather like the "twelve toes" of my September 10 dream, the two graphed lines showed six peaks mirroring each other somewhat. Later, on the six o'clock television news, I watched an odd combination of events: one was to do with the Statue of Liberty, which was being held by some antiwar veterans; the other was a filmed demonstration of psychokinesis by the Soviet sensitive Nina Kulagina. Watching this, in fact, triggered my memory of the September 10 dream that combined the Statue of Liberty with psychokinesis.

This dream correspondence with events of the day focused attention on the concept that ESP and PK may be part of a unitary process. Lewis's rather complex paper referred to acausality and Jung's theory of synchronicity: "Is it a coincidence that ESP involves an ordering of events where random disorder should obtain? I am suggesting that in some fundamental and mysterious way reality is not as random as it appears, and that ESP directly demonstrates this statistical fact."

My own interpretation of Lewis's data is that, in fact, what his machines were measuring was synchronicity; and that synchronicity fundamentally could be considered the basic "particle" of psi, including both ESP and PK. Or, put another way, our psychic fields interact with our environment to produce meaningful coincidences (synchronicity), some of which are mental (ESP) and some of which are physical (PK). This interaction is possible because of another dimension that our psychic fields can penetrate.

Could this interpenetration of the psychic universe with the physical universe be recorded somehow with instruments? It may be that the energy fields photographed by the Kirlian process will turn out to be related to the psychic fields to which I have been referring. One odd incident in my own life suggests that intense psychic fields may indeed be capable of visual measurement. On Easter Sunday 1972 I arranged for a parapsychological panel discussion at the science-fiction writers and fans convention, The Lunacon, in New York City. Seated at a table on either side of me were the parapsychologists Charles Honorton and Gertrude Schmeidler. I felt myself to be in an intensely activated psychic state. A friend was in the audience taking photos of the panel. When the photos were developed, they showed an odd consistency:

both Honorton and Dr. Schmeidler were in focus, but I, sitting between them and at the same distance from the camera, was always out of focus. This reminded me of an incident that Eileen Garrett had once told me about. When she had been photographed once, the developed photo showed not a trace of her. A similar incident had happened at the Conan Doyle Museum in London years ago. A group of men were assembled with a medium in an attempt to get a "spirit extra" photograph. When the photographer's plates were developed an hour or so later, they discovered that the medium had vanished from the picture. Just the empty chair remained where the medium had been sitting.

A television documentary made by the Germans of the American sensitive Ted Serios shows a somewhat startling effect. (You may recall that Ted's specialty was "thought photography," impressing images directly onto film.) As Ted went into his psychic state, in the process getting somewhat inebriated with a bottle of beer, he grimaced in effort and the television image began to blacken from around the outer edges. With a few more attempts, the image was blackened out altogether, and then, finally, there appeared in flashes another picture—a close representation of a target picture in a sealed envelope that he was attempting to reproduce. It may be that Ted's psychic field was becoming intensely activated to cause both the blackening out of the television image and the subsequent projection. Viewing the process in motion gives one the feeling that indeed some sort of fluctuating energy field is at work. Ted's "thoughtographic" techniques make use of both physical (PK) and mental (ESP) effects, since he must use ESP to discover what is in the sealed envelope and use PK to project it.

Although such remarkable control over psi processes is rare indeed, even average people can demonstrate the effects of their psi fields on each other. In numerous experiments with groups of people in psychic development classes and lectures, I often ask them to meditate on a target picture, either one that a person in another room is concentrating on (telepathy) or one that will be chosen at random after their images are recorded (precognition). Individuals are often quite successful in describing the target picture or some part of it. But the most striking effect that I have noticed is that the meditation imagery of the group contains many common elements not related to the target. Usually, these common elements are not distributed at random. A small group of people on one side of the room will all be seeing similar images, while another small group in another part of the room will report other images in common. Thus their seating relationship in the hall seems to determine somewhat the results they get. The audience seems to form collective pools of consciousness during meditation, organized spatially around key persons whose psi fields may be somewhat more active. A somewhat similar observation was made by the British researcher Sir Alister Hardy when he wrote me about a group ESP test. Some of the most striking correspondences in the ESP imagery pertained not to the target but to corresponding imagery of people near each other.

So, if indeed a sensitive's psi field enables him to penetrate the space-time continuum into another dimension—and if this hypothesis is confirmed by further experimentation—then we may have to treat more respectfully the writings of Spiritualism that describe another dimension.

If this other dimension were organized such that the "blueprint" of future events kept the same relative order as their actualization in our conscious world, then we would expect the most accurate precognitions to come with the shortest time intervals between dream and event; and conversely, we would expect distant events to be less accurate. But in the dream records of Christine Mylius and myself, kept over a period of years, this kind of relationship does not hold. Rather, the dream is usually triggered by some present event, and by association the dream describes the next encounter with a similar event—whether that be within days, weeks, months, or years. This relationship seems to indicate that the images of the unconscious are organized not temporally but symbolically. An analogy might be the subject headings in a library's card catalog. All the books on the same subject, regardless of date of publication, are listed together under the same heading—a condensed word symbol.

It is perfectly possible, of course, to focus or limit one's precognitive dreams to events of the very near future. Malcolm Bessent demonstrated this in his two precognitive dream studies. Many (perhaps even most) spontaneous precognitive dreams reported to parapsychologists pertain to events in the near future (retrospectively). But I would tend to put this down to the fact that the percipients do not regularly record their dreams and only recall one as being precognitive when they are reminded of it within a short period of time. Otherwise the dream memory fades quickly.

What might be the limits of prophecy? Only time—pierced by the psyche's invasion of another dimension—can tell.

9

The New Atlantis

One of the most fascinating patterns of prophecy to emerge in modern times is that of Atlantis, the fabled lost continent. Prophets have predicted that Atlantis will rise again, bringing up from the bottom of the sea evidence of its drowned civilization.

Edgar Cayce, America's "Sleeping Prophet," predicted that the rebirth of Atlantis would bring cataclysmic destruction to the coasts of America—"The New Atlantis."

Atlantis! The very name is redolent with the mystery and romance that have clung to it from milennia of speculation. Plato was the first to write of this mighty island kingdom in the Atlantic and the upheaval that sank it beneath the waves one night, twelve thousand years ago.

The ultimate source of the tale is an Egyptian priest, who had told the story to Solon, the great lawgiver of Athens. The priest chided the Greeks for knowing nothing of the destruction of the lost empire. But the Egyptians, he said, had complete records of Atlantis.

Atlantis lay west of the Pillars of Hercules [Gibraltar]. According to Plato, "The island was larger than Libya and Asia [the Middle East] put together, and from it could be reached other islands, and from the islands you might pass

through to the opposite continent [America?]." The priest
told how Atlantean aggressions in the Mediterranean had been
fought off by the ancient Athenians of nine thousand years
before. Then, in a single day and night, violent earthquakes
and floods destroyed the mighty Atlantean civilization. The
sea itself was unnavigable for many years because of the
impassable barrier of mud left behind by the lost continent.

In the Middle Ages the story of Atlantis was generally
believed. Francis Bacon drew on its rich tradition to write his
utopian fable, *The New Atlantis*, but the Age of Reason decided that speculation was getting out of hand and classified
Atlantis with Homer's Troy as ancient legend. Archaeology
discovered the reality of Troy, but Atlantis remains on the
shelf marked Myth.

Of the several thousand books on Atlantis perhaps the most
colorful are those written by cultists. Not satisfied with one
sunken continent, they have written of a sister continent in
the Pacific—called Lemuria or Mu. The name Lemuria was
first proposed by a nineteenth-century zoologist for a lost
continent in the Pacific that would account for the distribu-
tion of the lemur. Theosophists such as Madame Blavatsky and
Annie Besant were quick to write histories of the lost continent and its "root races." The "Sixth Root Race" is evolv-
ing now in Southern California and will migrate back to
Lemuria when it rises again and America sinks.

Mu (pronounced *moo*) was the ancient name for Lemuria,
claimed Col. James Churchward, whose book *The Lost Continent of Mu* was the first of a series written in the 1930s.
Churchward's sources were mysterious tablets kept in equally
mysterious Indian and Tibetan monasteries. According to
Churchward, Mu was the original garden of Eden where
the mother civilization flourished. Mu was wiped out by a
cataclysm about 11,500 years go—just before the destruction
of Atlantis.

That Atlantis was the original cradle of civilization was the theory offered by Ignatius Donnelly, a Congressman from Minnesota. In 1882 he published *Atlantis: The Antediluvian World*, in which he offered many ingenious explanations to prove that Plato's story was essentially right. He found in early American and European cultures many similarities that he explained as Atlantean in origin. He theorized that the biblical account of Noah and the flood reflected the memory of the destruction of Atlantis.

In 1883 the complete vaporization of the volcanic island of Krakatoa—the most tremendous explosion of modern times—dramatized the possibility of an island's sudden destruction and sent people hustling to the bookshops for Donnelly's book. It is still the most popular and influential book ever written on Atlantis.

An English statesman, the great Prime Minister William Gladstone, was profoundly impressed by Donnelly's arguments and attempted to convince his cabinet to back an expedition to search for Atlantis's sunken towers at the bottom of the Atlantic.

Not until 1966 was a full-fledged expedition sent out to search for Atlantis—this time in the Aegean. That inspiration came from Prof. Anghelos Galanopoulos, a leading Greek seismologist who had always been fascinated with the legend of Atlantis. Galanopoulos suggested that Plato's geography was off, that Plato was also off by a factor of ten in his date for the destruction, and that Plato dropped another decimal point in his estimate of the size of Atlantis. Galanopoulos agreed with Plato that the island kingdom had a moat around it.

A submerged moat encircling the ancient Minoan island Thera (now Santorin) was subsequently discovered. Thera was two-thirds submerged by a volcanic eruption in 1400 B.C.—four times as destructive as that of Krakatoa in 1883. The

Greek-American team termed their discovery "most convincing proof" that they had found Atlantis.

The noted novelist, poet, and scholar Robert Graves agrees with many modern theorists on Atlantis that the legend might be the distorted memory of the inundation of some ancient coastal city. Graves has found just such a city in Libya. It was located on Lake Tritonis but was submerged by an earthquake upheaval, as described by an ancient Roman travel-writer, Diodorus of Sicily. Conveniently, that city's name was also Atlantis.

Most occult and psychic sources place Atlantis in the Atlantic Ocean. The most prolific and well-documented of these sources comes from the trance readings of the American psychic Edgar Cayce, given in the 1930s and early 1940s. Of the 14,000 recorded transcripts af Cayce's psychic readings on file at the Association of Research and Enlightenment in Virginia Beach, Virginia, more than 700 contain references to Atlantis. In the Cayce readings Atlantis emerges as a technological civilization in some ways more advanced than our own. It flourished over a span of thousands of years, survived two partial destructions that broke it into islands, but was completely destroyed about 11,000 years ago.

Although similar accounts appear in occult literature dating from the 1890s, Cayce's friends and family testify that this simple photographer with only an eighth-grade education read nothing more occult than the Bible. In trance, however, he claimed access to the Universal Unconscious—the timeless and spaceless world of images—past, present, and future. And it was presumably this Universal Unconscious that furnished information about Atlantis in context of his readings about former lives in Atlantis.

Alleged spirit communication was the source for Joseph Leslie's *Submerged Atlantis Restored*, published in America in 1911. Leslie was a Rochester, New York, spiritualist who claimed to be in contact with Atlantean spirits for thirty years. From his "spirit interviews" he reconstructed the entire Atlantean civilization: its history, literature, art, music, and technology. As an added benefit for serious Atlantean scholars who may want to check his sources, he gives language instruction in "Atlantean."

Leslie's history of Atlantis agrees with Cayce in depicting its three destructions, though with different dates. As with some occult sources, he and Cayce picture groups of refugees making their way from the destroyed Atlantis to Egypt and Yucatan, where they built pyramids—we are unnerved to find from Cayce—with the aid of antigravity devices. Cayce also claimed that the Atlanteans had left behind enormous power plants that drew energy from the sun to guide their ships, submarines, and . . . aircraft.

A description of an Atlantean aircraft was furnished Leslie in 1893 by an alleged Atlantean entity, "Yer-mah," who bragged about being the daredevil pilot of a *Telta Aeta* ("Atlantean" for "airplane"). Made from an aluminum-like material in the shape of an eagle, the craft was powered by electricity drawn from the atmosphere and could transport up to one hundred passengers. Its normal cruising speed was between 75 and 100 miles per hour, but it was sometimes taken up to 150 miles per hour by daredevils like Leslie's friend "Yer-mah."

"Yer-mah's" break through the credibility barrier is matched by a recent breakthrough in cartography. Certain old maps, undoubtedly copies of far more ancient ones, show Antarctic mountain ranges that have been covered with ice for thousands of years. Antarctica was only discovered in the nineteenth century, and indeed, these mountain ranges were found only in the last few years.

The idea that pre–Ice Age Antarctica appeared in certain medieval maps was first proposed by Capt. A. H. Mallery in a Georgetown University radio forum in 1956. He drew attention to the Piri Re'is map compiled by a Turkish admiral of that name in 1513. Further research was undertaken under the direction of Prof. Charles H. Hapgood at New Hampshire State University and in 1966 he published proof of Mallery's theory in *Maps of the Ancient Sea Kings* (Chilton, 1966). Air Force map experts agree that pre–Ice Age Antarctica is accurately mapped; says Lt. Col. Harold Z. Ohlmeyer, "The ice cap in this region is now about a mile thick. We have no idea how the data on this map can be reconciled with the supposed state of geographical knowledge in 1513."

Professor Hapgood speculates that the lost civilization that drew the originals must have been as nearly advanced as our own. Captain Mallery thinks that the accuracy of the maps may have been achieved with the aid of aerial surveys.

These remarkable maps have reached us through generations of recopying by sailors up until medieval times. Ironically, scholars of medieval universities knew nothing of these maps and taught their students with far inferior ones. Only recently has cartography advanced to a stage equal to that proven to exist before the Ice Age.

Of those pre–Ice Age cartographers, nothing is known. All that we actually know is that suddenly—11,000 years ago—the Ice Age ended. Torrents of ice and snow raged from melting ice caps to raise the sea level about 300 feet. If any ancient cities ringed those surging seas, they would have perished without a trace.

One provocative trace, however, was discovered in 1965. During excavation for a new apartment house on the Riviera, a bulldozer unearthed remains of an older house—*very* old—200,000 years old.[1] It was oval-shaped, roughly fifty feet by twenty, and was supported by upright beams. Before this discovery, scientists had thought that pre-Neanderthal peoples lived in the open or in caves. It was only 20,000 years ago that man was painting on the walls of caves in France and

Spain. A hundred empires could have risen and fallen in the intervening 180,000 years. What had man been doing since he built his first summer home on the Riviera?

Having so little evidence, scientists can only guess. Psychics, however, are not daunted by lack of evidence. Here is Edgar Cayce's description of an event of 50,722 B.C.:

> In Atlantis the entity attended the meeting of many representatives of many countries to devise ways of dealing with the great animals overruning the earth. Means were devised to change environs suitable for beasts. This was administered by sending out death rays or super cosmic rays from various central plants. These rays will be discovered within the next twenty-five years.[2]

Death rays capable of killing giant mastadons have been imaginatively featured in science-fiction thrillers for years. But now the movies have one that actually works: the laser, a coherent light beam that can cut through diamond and reduce slabs of marble to dust. It was invented in 1958, just twenty-five years after Cayce gave that reading in 1933.

Since that time other discoveries have been made that might throw a light on the mystery of Atlantis. In the middle of the Atlantic scientists discovered a vast submerged mountain range that stretches the length of the ocean. Evidence that this mid-Atlantic ridge was above water hundreds of thousands of years ago is strong; evidence that it was above water when Atlantis allegedly flourished is slight. Only the remains of a few fresh-water plants that grew more than 10,000 years ago support the legend of Atlantis. A weak foundation for an empire.

Evidence for an empire in the Pacific was first discovered in 1966. While probing the depths of the ocean fifty miles off the coast of Peru for specimens of a rare living-fossil mollusk, Dr. Robert Menzies of Duke University discovered by accident something much more astonishing: strange columns standing upright in the ooze, 6,000 feet under the sea. They had been carved out of rock. Enigmatic hieroglyphics deepen the mystery. Dr. Menzies's comment was: "We do not find structures like these anywhere else. I have never seen anything like this before."

Are these columns remains of a destroyed temple of Mu, the lost continent of the Pacific? For an answer, we shall have to wait until a research submarine can be sent down to take a closer look. In view of the controversy between Peru and the United States on offshore fishing rights, that may well be many years from now.

For a closer look at the lost continent of Atlantis, we shouldn't have long to wait either—if Edgar Cayce is right. Here is what he prophesied:

"Poseidia will be among the first portions of Atlantis to rise again—expect it in '68 and '69—not so far away." Cayce claimed that the sunken Atlantean island of Poseidia is located near the Bahamas and that its reemergence from the sea will uncover the ancient ruins of an Atlantean temple. So far there has been no sudden uprush of land in the Atlantic, but a prophet's dates seldom can pinpoint events in time. Yet Cayce did seem to pinpoint a location where some extraordinary archaeological findings came to light in 1968. Sunken columns and pavements made of gigantic blocks of stone were first seen under the water off the coast of Bimini in 1965 by the archaeologist Pino Turrolla. In 1968 several underwater expeditions discovered additional artifacts.

I am told by author Ruth Hagy Brod, who is writing a book on Turrolla's discoveries, that he has discovered additional ruins of the same civilization on the South American continent, including artifacts that can be dated by scientific means. Perhaps, at last, some scientifically solid evidence can be verified.

Any day now, if Cayce is right, we can expect to find in Egypt, near the Sphinx, a lost pyramid containing not only records of Atlantis but also prophecies for our own time. According to a late Egyptologist, Dr. J. O. Kinnaman, the last survivor of the famed King Tut expedition, Atlantean records may also be found in a secret chamber of the Great Pyramid at Gizeh. Toward the end of his life in 1961, Kinnaman claimed that he and famed British Egyptologist Sir William Flinders Petrie had discovered that chamber but were persuaded by Egyptian officials to swear an oath of secrecy— as the world was not yet ready for the knowledge that the Atlanteans had built the pyramid. I should be somewhat happier with this story if it had appeared in a scientific journal instead of a Rosicrucian publication.

Edgar Cayce specifically said that the Great Pyramid had no secret chamber. He was apparently right, although it took $500,000 to prove it. Dr. Luis Alvarez, a Nobel-prize-winning physicist, cooperated with Egyptian officials to "X-ray" the Great Pyramid with cosmic rays in hopes of discovering such a secret chamber. They couldn't find one. But no matter. The Smithsonian Institution, the National Geographic Society, and others have extended Dr. Alvarez's group another $750,000 to try the Pyramid of Chephren. If, by chance, they should be successful in their quest it would be a small price to pay. Egyptologists, incidentally, date the Pyramid of Chephren at about 4,600 years old; the Great Pyramid had been built by his father, Cheops. These dates, of course, are thousands of years at variance with those given by Cayce.

In Cayce's prophecies about the rising of Atlantis, his timing related to other earth changes. The earliest such prophecy listed by Edgar Evans Cayce, one of Cayce's sons, in his book *Edgar Cayce on Atlantis* (Hawthorn, 1963), was April 9, 1932. In response to the question "How soon will the changes in the earth's activity begin to be apparent?"

Cayce replied: "When there is the first breaking-up of some conditions in the South Sea (that's South Pacific, to be sure), and those as apparent in the sinking or arising of that which is almost opposite to it, or in the Mediterranean, and the Aetna area. Then we may know it has begun."

Further details were given in 1934: "As to the changes physical again: the earth will be broken up in the western portion of America. The greater portion of Japan will go into the sea. The upper portion of Europe will be changed as in the twinkling of an eye. Land will appear off the east coast of America."

And again in 1941: "In the next few years, lands will appear in the Atlantic as well as in the Pacific. And what is the coast line now of many a land will be bed of the ocean. . . .

"Portions of the now east coast of New York, or New York City itself, will in the main disappear. This will be in another generation, though, here; while the southern portions of Carolina, Georgia, these will disappear. This will be much sooner."

Other readings placed these earth changes in the general period 1958–1998, culminating in a shifting of the earth's poles by the year 2001. Such phrases as "the twinkling of an eye" to describe a geographical change in northern Europe suggest a catastrophe unprecedented in man's memory; yet elsewhere Cayce denied that the changes would be catastrophic. When asked whether the rising of Atlantis would "cause a sudden convolution," Cayce replied: "In 1998 we may find a great deal of the activities as have been wrought by the gradual changes that are coming about. . . . This is a gradual, not a cataclysmic activity in the experience of the earth in this period."

The great variance between Cayce's readings on this subject may indicate that he really wasn't sure about any dates. Going from "Expect it in '68 or '69 . . ." to "In 1998 . . . gradual changes . . ." gives a wide latitude of interpretation. Some Cayce interpreters, such as Jess Stearn in his book *Edgar Cayce—The Sleeping Prophet* (Doubleday, 1966), wax wildly enthusiastic on Cayce's prophetic accuracy ("incredibly high, close to one hundred percent"). My own reaction, however, after studying a number of Cayce's records at Virginia Beach is that most of his prophecies are given in such an oracular way as to make any kind of evaluation strictly a matter of subjective feeling. Cayce's convoluted language makes even comprehension, much less evaluation, difficult.

Of another prophet of our time, absolutely nothing is known, not even his real name. Writing under the pseudonym of Dino Kraspedon, a Brazilian living in São Paulo wrote a strange book in 1958 entitled *My Contact with Flying Saucers*. His English publisher, Neville Armstrong, suspects that Kraspedon might be a schoolteacher. Appallingly or appealingly, depending on one's reaction to stories of saucer contactees, Kraspedon attributes his prophecies to the captain of a flying saucer. He, like Cayce, predicted the tilting of the earth's axis but gave as a cause a warming of the North Polar ice cap that would redistribute the earth's waters. In his words: "I believe it could happen sometime between 1968 and 1972. It will be brought home to you by a tremendous earthquake that will shake the earth to its foundations. Cities will fall in ruins and great cracks will appear in the surface of the Earth. . . . When this happens land will emerge from the Pacific and from the North and South Atlantic. The emergence of these new land masses will change the level of the oceans, causing flooding in the low-lying countries."

Kraspedon's time limit has just run out. But the concept of axis-tilting is as popular as ever. Could Kraspedon possibly have heard of Cayce's prophecy made years before? I doubt it, since writings about Cayce were not in print in Brazil in the 1950s. But perhaps there is an occult underground that goes beyond language, for in 1950 a Brazilian medium named Hercilio Maes published a tract allegedly dictated to him by his spirit guide "Ramatis." Quoted in Pedro McGregor's *Jesus of the Spirits* (1967), Maes prophesies that the earth's axis will change through ninety degrees due to the gravitational pull of an enormous new planet which will enter our system soon. "Entire continents such as Europe will be completely destroyed and vanish forever beneath the new oceans which will form. North and South Poles will be totally de-iced and man will find unimaginable riches to help him form the new humanity of the Third Millennium."

Axis-tilting also appears in a prophecy from 1922 quoted by Harriette and Homer Curtiss in their *Coming World Changes* (1926). The prophecy was given them by a mysterious personage who immodestly titled himself the King of the World: ". . . owing to volcanic activity *and a tilting of the axis of the Earth*, vast and cataclysmic changes were to take place in the comparatively near future which would entirely remodel and rearrange the land surface of the globe."

As leaders of the Order of Christian Mystics, the Curtisses drew much inspiration from Madame Blavatsky's *The Secret Doctrine*, which prophesies: "That the periodical sinking and reappearance of mighty continents, now called Atlantean and Lemurian by modern writers, is no fiction will be demonstrated. It is only in the twentieth century that portions, if not the whole, of the present work will be vindicated."

The unconventional Immanuel Velikovsky, who has provoked bitter controversy in scientific circles with his best-selling books, uncovered a wealth of geological evidence for a theory that ice ages were caused by a sudden tilting of the earth's axis. Coral once grew at the North Pole and tropical rain forests petrified to coal in Antarctica. Ice Age glaciers visited Africa below the equator but did not come to Siberia, now the coldest spot in the world. Mammoths frozen so quickly that their flesh is edible thousands of years later provide Velikovsky evidence for an incredibly swift climate change.

Velikovsky's axis-tilt theory is only one of his theories of catastrophe. His other theories have been gaining supporters recently because of new discoveries in space that confirm some of his early predictions. Venus, as he predicted, has been found to rotate retrograde and is very hot. Now in his seventies, Velikovsky thinks that the age of natural catastrophe is over. In an address given in 1966, he gave a new warning "even at the price of appearing again a prophet of doom." Mankind, he says, harbors in its collective soul the memory of these horrendous events and seems to be seeking to match them with the development of weapons that can lay waste to the planet. In the 1970s, Velikovsky sounds very conventional.

Another theorist, who started out unconventional and is staying that way, is Emil Sepic of Eureka, California. By dint of "40 years of interest in the earth's motions and 12 years of intensive study and research," Sepic has been able to calculate that the earth's axis will tilt by 1978, bringing worldwide flooding and destruction. Not claiming preferential status, Sepic dourly comments that "we are all in this together."

Although Sepic's voice appears to call from the wilderness of crackpot science, from the "in" scientists at Columbia University's Lamont Geological Observatory comes a tantalizing study that proves that the magnetic poles of the earth have reversed many times. They have *not* suggested that the poles have reversed physically along with the magnetic change. In their words: "Over the past 75 million years the earth's field has on the average reversed about once every million years. One may note that for the past 20 million years the average interval between reversals has been about 250,000 years, that the largest interval has been 800,000 years and that occasionally the interval was no more than 10,000 years. The next reversal would therefore seem to be due."

In the geological time scale *due* may mean many thousand years or so from now, so no need to throw away your old compass. If the magnetic poles *should* reverse, however, it would momentarily collapse the earth's protective magnetic fields, exposing the world's populace to deadly radiation—perhaps more deadly than any catastrophic flood prophesied by others.

Probably the oldest prophecy considered to predict a tilting of the earth's axis is by the world's most famous prophet, Nostradamus, the sixteenth-century French seer who predicted even his own fame. He didn't give the year, but he did give the month for this cataclysmic event: "There shall be in the month of October, a great revolution made, such that everybody will think that the earth has lost its natural motion and has gone down into perpetual darkness."

Nostradamus didn't specify the consequences of that "great revolution," but elsewhere he does warn of "great inundations" scheduled before the "universal conflagration." Before and after the inundations he predicted "burning stones shall fall from Heaven."

The most spectacular "burning stones" that fall from the skies are the Leonid meteor showers, which appeared most recently in November 1966 and will return next in 1999— an apocalyptic year for the prophets.

A now-forgotten religious prophet, Dr. Paulus, in the style of the Old Testament prophets gave no year for the destruction awaiting New York City because of its wickedness; and where others would find "The New Atlantis" he found "The New California." In Paulus's small book of prophecies published in 1869, the last page is obviously the most important one because it is printed in red.

"For after having destroyed the city of New York by

earthquakes, and raised from the mysterious deep, by the same commotions, 'THE NEW CALIFORNIA,' a land of gold, for the natural use of His faithful,—He will build up through His grace, on the golden land, a new city for His faithful of America. . . . And thousands of ye true-hearted, noble Americans will flock to it. . . . And peace and harmony will reign in the New City of the Lord."

If the next prophet is right, several "New Cities of the Lord" will be required for displaced "true-hearted, noble Americans " living on the East Coast.

John Pendragon, pseudonym of a Brtish clairvoyant who writes a monthly prediction column for the British *Fate* magazine, predicts that: "The cities of the Atlantic coast from Boston to Baltimore will be wiped out, the nexus of this annihilation being New York, Pittsburgh, and Philadelphia, with severe repercussions on all areas within 500 miles of New York City. I do not see cities remaining, but rather the sites of them, mostly under water. . . . Look ahead, 15, 20 or more years. I name no specific dates. The danger is there, and if it is ignored, the catastrophe will be *immense*."

Pendragon's vision of the East Coast destruction may well have been influenced by Cayce's now world-famous prophecies. The shadow of Cayce may also be glimpsed in the predictions for 1968 given by Jeane Dixon: "In this century the over-population of the planet by mankind is not going to be a problem. Something literally earth-shattering will occur, a natural phenomenon which I believe will be divine intervention, something like a meteor. It will happen in a matter of minutes and will involve the shifting of the waters of the earth."

In her book *My Life and Prophecies* (Morrow, 1969), Mrs. Dixon predicts that a comet will hit the earth in the mid-1980s, causing earthquakes and tidal waves from the ocean in which it will land. If Mrs. Dixon has in mind Halley's comet—due for a return visit in 1985—then it would be indeed surprising, since a comet is mainly composed of gas. Meteors would be more likely to cause such havoc.

A seeress who foreshadowed by several years Cayce's prophecies of Atlantis was a German medium known as the Dresden Pythia. In her prophecies of August 1919, published in 1920, she predicted a great war between Japan and America, and a new European world war. Apparently her patriotism overshadowed her prophetic accuracy, for she predicted that Germany would be the victor over France and England.

We may presume that postwar German resentment against the French and English also colored this prophecy:

> Part of the French, Belgian, and German coasts will be flooded. All of England will sink into the sea during a terrible earthquake. . . . At the same time there will be a reemergence of a great continent in the region of the Azores (the old Atlantis). There will be found traces of an ancient culture. Also at other places will new land emerge from the sea.
>
> A world destruction as happened to Atlantis 11,000 years ago. . . . Instead of Atlantis, all of England and parts of the northwest European coasts will sink into the sea. And in contrast, the sunken Azores region, the island of Poseidonis, will again be raised from the sea.

The question of whether Poseidonis, or Poseidia, is in the region of the Bahamas, as Cayce claimed, or near the Azores, as the Dresden Pythia claimed, I shall leave to students of the occult. They may also be interested in a German novel of 1924 in which the rising of Atlantis floods France. Again, resentment against a conquering nation seems to inspire the prophecy. To balance the global picture, an Englishman, Lewis Spence, wrote during World War II a book, *Will*

Europe Follow Atlantis?, in which he predicted that the tilting of the earth's axis would cause the European continent to sink—a punishment for her wickedness.

Sometimes scholars of prophecy get so zealous that one suspects them of using student April Fool jokes as documentation to their cause. Georg Lomer's *Coming World Catastrophes*, published in Germany in 1921, cites a Harvard University study to prove his point that Atlantis has started to rise. Two Harvard professors made a study of the sea bottom in the western part of the Atlantic Ocean in 1912 and concluded that the seabed had undergone a significant rise. Either Lomer was taken in by some student joke, or those professors really do bear the singularly unfortunate names of Dr. Liar and Dr. Deluder.

The names may be a joke, but the facts are not: oceanographic studies currently being carried out show that the Mid-Atlantic Ridge is being very slowly forced up by heat from the earth's interior. A portion of it was violently thrust up over 3,000 feet by an earthquake in 1960, and other parts have given birth to volcanic islands even more recently. If the next prophet is right, earthquakes will force up ancient Atlantean islands.

Cheiro (pronounced kí-ro) was the pseudonym of Count Louis Hamon, a British astrologer, palmist, and clairvoyant who became world famous for his successful predictions for the glittering personalities of two generations ago. In retirement by 1925, he wrote *Cheiro's World Predictions* (London: Herbert Jenkins), published in 1927, in which he prophesied that Germany and Italy would war with France and England. Rather oddly, he predicted that London would be partially destroyed by *Russian* airplanes. One wonders what details will be wrong in this prophecy:

> During the coming 50 years an earthquake zone will develop in a North Easterly direction from the Pacific Coast

of Peru, passing through Panama and Mexico, through the
Northern States and Canada to the Arctic regions.

Eastern cities of North America . . . will be seriously
affected and a considerable part of New York will be
destroyed. . . .

During the next fifty to a hundred years after a series of
devastating earthquakes, the islands of the Azores will rise
from the Atlantic and the ruins of the long lost continent of
Atlantis will be discovered and explored.

The present-day North Atlantic islands of the Azores are
located with uncanny precision on the Piri Re'is Map of
1513. But seekers of long-lost islands will find one on that
remarkable map 700 miles off the coast of Brazil. This unknown island is depicted as having coastal highlands and a
central plain; its coastline is detailed with inlets and offshore
islands, not smooth as mythical islands were typically depicted
in medieval maps. Where only the tiny points of Peter and
Paul jut out from the sea now, it lies over a portion of the
submerged Mid-Atlantic Ridge. That may be a coincidence,
or it may be . . . Atlantis.

Although Atlantis may have long since vanished, we still
have Atlanteans. They belong to a group called The Atlanteans, founded in England by Helio-Arcanophus, alleged to
be ancient Atlantean royalty who manifests through the
trance mediumship of Anthony Neate. Neate, or rather
Helio-Arcanophus, gives periodic trance lectures in London's
Vegetarian Hall to the assembled faithful. His lectures range
from ancient history, astrology, flying saucers, and healing to
prophecies of the future. He delivered this prophecy in 1957:

Events will work up gradually. There will be earthquakes
where they are not normally experienced; volcanoes will
become active which have been extinct for centuries. Ab-
normal weather conditions will prevail, getting worse as

time progresses. The seasons will appear to have no more significance, for there will be warm days in winter months and cold days during the normally warm periods of your year. As the time nears there will be increasing darkness, for the rays of the sun will be blocked out. A substance commonly known as "black rain" will fall from the skies and there will be considerable chaos. When these events have risen to a crescendo, the Earth will tilt. Many lands will disappear beneath the boiling seas and some will rise from their watery resting places. Among the latter will be the Island Continent of Atlantis, a land which never completed its evolution and will soon return to do so.

As for the time of these events, Helio-Arcanophus says: "Within most of your lifetimes; for your children will rule Atlantis."

There are no earlier prophecies by which to judge that prophet, and indeed, Mr. Neate's credentials as a medium are highly suspect. The next prophet, however, is probably the most thoroughly tested medium in modern times.

Through the mediumship of Eileen J. Garrett, prophecies of Atlantis were given in the 1920s. Although Mrs. Garrett had many precognitions in her own right—the most dramatic being of the destruction of the *Airship R 101* in 1930—she had no memory of what her trance personalities said, nor did she claim responsibility for them. Here, then, is an excerpt from a séance attended by Dr. Abraham Wallace and Sir Arthur Conan Doyle, published in R. H. Saunders's *Health* (1928), in which "Abduhl Latif," a trance personality concerned principally with healing, prophesied on Atlantis:

> *Sir Arthur Conan Doyle:* Can you give any approximate date for the sinking of Atlantis?"
>
> *Abduhl Latif:* ". . . It is not really true to say that the Atlantian people could not make records. Many of these records will one day be found by you, and there must have been

something like 15,000 or 16,000 years from the time of my own life [12th Century] to that of the lost races of the Atlantian Civilization. Many people will tell you that Atlantis disappeared so quickly. That is not true. There was a series of three cataclysmic eruptions that caused the gradual disappearance of land. . . .

". . . there are great monuments, tombs to be opened, there will be cataclysms that will bring up to you from the bottom of the sea that which I swear in the name of Almighty God to be true. . . ."

Dr. Abraham Wallace: "I was told that in the early days they had airships, and they drove their ships by means of [etheric] energy."

Abduhl Latif: "I do not say that they had airships, but they had means of flying; they also had means of producing light from the etheric force, which is equivalent today to the electric energy."

Dr. Abraham Wallace: "I understand that the utilization of that etheric energy for evil purposes was the cause of the first catastrophe in Atlantis, and that today, on the Continent, there are some people who have attained to a certain knowledge of that, and if they utilize it as they propose to do there will be a tremendous catastrophe. . . ."

Abduhl Latif: "I assure you of this: that you are quite right in what you hear of the possibility of cataclysmic catastrophe. As soon as a nation, be it great or small, attains a certain degree of knowledge, that knowledge is very often a two-edged sword in the hands of ignorance. . . ." [3]

A sobering prophecy, one that reminds us that Germany had initiated work on nuclear fission, though it was the Americans, of course, who developed the energy capable of world destruction. Cayce also elaborated on the theme that a destruction of Atlantis was caused by the misuse of powerful energies. Abduhl Latif agrees with Cayce, the Dresden Pythia, and Cheiro in prophesying a rediscovery of Atlantean ruins as well as the familar catastrophe.

It is curious that Sir Arthur Conan Doyle did not question Abduhl Latif further about the "cataclysmic catastrophe," for Sir Arthur had been receiving similar communications from his own alleged control, "Pheneas," and from American and English mediums since 1923. Shortly before his death in 1930, he wrote a letter, published in the *London Sunday Express* (July 20, 1930), summarizing the messages:

> If we state the course of events as outlined in these various documents and check them with our own information the result is overwhelming. It would entail a period of terrific natural convulsions during which a large portion of the human race would perish. Earthquakes of great severity, enormous tidal waves would seem to be the agents. There is mention of war, but that would appear to be only in the early stages and to be in some way the signal for the crisis.
>
> The following general details may be gathered:—
>
> That the crisis will come in an instant;
>
> That the general destruction and utter dislocation of civilised life will be beyond belief;
>
> That there will be a short period of utter chaos followed by some reconstruction;
>
> That the total period of the upheavals will be roughly three years;
>
> That the chief centres of disturbance will be the Eastern Mediterranean basin, where not less than five countries will entirely disappear.
>
> Also the Atlantic, where there will be a rise of land which will be a cause of those waves which will bring about great disasters upon the Americans, the Irish, and the Western European shore, involving all the low-lying British coasts. There are indicated further great upheavals in the Southern Pacific and in the Japanese region.

That prophecy surely surpasses in bizarreness the adventures of Conan Doyle's fictional hero, Sherlock Holmes. Although Sir Arthur felt the time for these events was "very close," he also said that mankind could be saved by returning to spiritual values, a sentiment similar to that expressed by Cayce.

With more than a million copies of books in print about Edgar Cayce, it is no wonder that his prophecies are so widely known; very few people, however, realize that there were other prophets of Atlantis, that Cayce's predictions fit into a far larger prophetic context. Many of Cayce's predictions concerning Atlantis and earth changes formed part of an occult tradition that goes back at least a century. It was especially strong in the Theosophical Society, founded by Madame Blavatsky, and can be glimpsed in nearly every Spiritualistic group that flourished earlier this century. None of the prophets quoted in this chapter make reference to prophecies of others that might be influencing them. Yet there can be little doubt that such influence plays an important role much as it does in literary traditions. There is also the possibility of influence by ESP from other minds.

If we accept Cayce's explanation of a Universal Unconscious as the source for his predictions, then it might be a good idea to consider briefly what the Universal Unconscious might consist of. I believe Cayce once described it (perhaps metaphorically) as a great library with thought records from all who have ever lived. If this great library is like worldly libraries, then the age of the books will make little difference in certain important areas. The dialogues of Plato are as relevant now as ever. The great religious books of the world still find readers seeking after wisdom. But when it comes to science books, only the most recent have much value. I once read a geography book from 1799 that contained scarcely a single correct statement in it. The ancient Roman Pliny wrote a book on natural history that has incredibly inaccurate howlers in it. One must read such a book with great selectivity. It may be, too, that the Universal Unconscious has every thought from man's history—many of which are inaccurate—and that we must select them as carefully as we separate myths from reality.

If myths are primitive history, and I think they are, then the myth of Atlantis may one day be shown to have historical roots. The explorations off the coast of Bimini and South America seem to me the most likely to provide such evidence of a relatively advanced pre–Ice Age civilization. Atlantis has yet another reality, however, that of a powerful archetype in the unconscious: an advanced civilization destroyed by its misuse of technology. Cayce's predictions of future earth changes always came in the context of Atlantis: As it was then, so shall it be again. A surprisingly large number of other prophets also link their predictions of catastrophic earth changes to a rising of Atlantis.

America, already marked by Francis Bacon centuries ago as "The New Atlantis," seems the focus of these predictions. The big question, obviously, is do the predictions have any validity, and if so, how much?

Indeed, that was the question that sparked my research into these predictions in 1966. A Ouija board prophecy said that New York would be flooded in 1973; a few days later I read of Cayce's predictions; and shortly afterward, came upon the Kraspedon prediction of an axis-tilt that would cause flooding by 1972. Yet in late 1968, when in a hypnotic state, I saw that flooding would come from Eastern rivers swollen by rain in 1972 and 1973. There were disastrous floods in 1972, but the seeming catastrophe had been scaled down. Perhaps, in the same way, these other prophecies have been considerably overdramatized. Events of fifty years seen to happen in a few minutes represent unnatural catastrophe. But when slowed down to their natural speed of geologic time, they become less dramatic—more "natural," if you like.

Yet there lurks the possibility of some great convolution, possibly toward the end of the century, that may change the face of the earth. If the archetype of Atlantis is completely fulfilled in reality, then, whether by natural or man-made forces, America may indeed become "The New Atlantis."

10

The Earthquake Sweepstakes

When I told my friends I was moving from New York to California in 1973, the usual response was, "Aren't you afraid California is going to fall into the sea? That's what Edgar Cayce predicted."

My reply was, "Edgar Cayce never predicted that California would go into the sea." But I generally added, "I wouldn't be surprised if there were some mild earthquakes. I've seen some in my dreams."

Here is a dream I had on August 26, 1971: "Suddenly the walls in one room [of a house] began to crumble as something came through it. The room began to tremble. I realized it was an earthquake. I ran downstairs and out onto the street to watch. As I looked around I was surprised that none of the buildings were falling, although they were swaying. At the end of the road there was a large crater partially filled with water. It may have been left there by construction workers. But the road seemed to vibrate like a ribbon, and the crater with the sloshing water would rise up and fall down. It was a spectacular effect."

My analysis of the dream was: "May be partially precognitive of an earthquake I shall witness one day. . . . Since I am planning to go to the West Coast, it is more logical for it to be there."

In a way, I think watching an earthquake might be very exciting. But not, of course, if California was dropping into the sea. The rumor that Edgar Cayce predicted such a fate for California can probably be traced back to a pamphlet first published in 1959 by the Association for Research and Enlightenment. Entitled *Earth Changes*, it was written by an anonymous geologist who examined Cayce's predictions of earth changes. One well-known prophecy reads: "If there are the greater activities in the Vesuvius, or Pelee, then the southern coast of California—and the areas between Salt Lake and the southern portions of Nevada—may expect, within the three months following same, an inundation by the earthquakes."

The geologist speculated that "perhaps the 'inundation' of the southern coast of California . . . refers to an inundation by tsunami (a tidal wave). . . . Or perhaps by *inundation*, an overwhelming number of earthquakes is implied."

When Cayce's prophecy was quoted by Mei Ling in her book *World Prophecy* in 1963, the word *caused* is inserted so as to read, "an inundation (caused) by the earthquakes." Mei Ling also quoted a Dr. E. R. Lindsey of the Four Square Gospel Tabernacle in Sacramento as predicting for the year 1969: "An earthquake will shake the whole earth. Land slippage will begin in the San Andreas fault in California and the major part of California will go into the Pacific Ocean."

The modified prophecy gained currency in occult circles in Southern California and made its way north.

As students of San Francisco earthquake lore well remember, the Great Quake and fire of 1906 happened on April 18. The reportedly computer-derived date for a big quake offered by a Haight-Ashbury personality, Beau Maverick, fell precisely at 8:19 A.M. on April 19, 1969. Another popular time offered by various occult types was 3:13 P.M. on April 4, reminiscent of the Good Friday earthquake in Alaska in 1964. As these and other prophecies gained currency, the Central Premonitions Registry in New York began to be inundated by California earthquake predictions—and the Earthquake Sweepstakes was on.

An enterprising author named Curt Gentry picked April 1969 as the "fictional" doomsday date for the Great Earthquake in his book, *The Last Day of the Late, Great State of California*. Strategically, he made his television appearances to publicize the book on the *East* Coast during the month of April 1969.

Not to be outdone, the mayor of San Francisco, John Alioto, imaginatively affirmed his faith that San Francisco would survive the Earthquake Sweepstakes. He announced a gigantic Earthquake Party for 5:13 A.M. on April 18—the sixty-third anniversary of the Great Quake of 1906—at the Civic Center Plaza. Several thousand people attended to celebrate their defiance of what was called later San Francisco's most publicized nonevent of 1969. At precisely 5:13 A.M. the crowd watched San Francisco engulfed once more in earthquake and fire, as portrayed in the old Hollywood film *San Francisco*. Once again, Clark Gable came to the rescue of Jeanette MacDonald.

Prophets started coming out of the woodwork to make their stab at a date. Here are a few registered with the Central Premonitions Registry:

• "June 18, 1969—Earthquake wipes out San Francisco and Los Angeles and several Manhattan blocks followed by social war."

• "September 1969—Massive quakes in California, tidal waves, devastation to Washington State down to Mexico."

• "June 28, 1969, or July 28—California quake."

- "August 1969—Totally devastating earthquake throughout California. Tidal wave will affect South America."
- "June 12, 1969—Extremely heavy quake on Pacific Coast with heavy loss of life."
- "June 5 or June 6, 1969—Earthquake in California."
- "September 1969 or before—Catastrophe in California. Half million dead."

Meanwhile, in California, scientists at the California Institute of Technology in Pasadena felt it necessary to deny the rumors in a press release: "Wild predictions of disastrous earthquakes—issued by self-proclaimed oracles and other visionaries—are not supported by scientific evidence and are frightening many Californians needlessly."

Scientists indulge, however, in their own brand of earthquake scare. "San Francisco almost wiped out, millions of casualties, rescue operations paralyzed by the destruction of the Golden Gate and Oakland bridges . . ." might be the aftermath of a catastrophic earthquake now imminent in Central California, warned University of Michigan physicist Dr. Peter A. Franken. The San Andreas Fault, a deep split in the earth's crust running the length of California, causes an earthquake roughly every fifty years. It is now overdue, having built up an alarming amount of strain since the San Francisco Quake of 1906 and the Los Angeles Quake of 1857.

"The big earthquake might not come for twenty years," says Dr. Franken, "but it could be tomorrow."

A less frightening, but quite accurate, prediction was published on January 17, 1971, in the *National Enquirer*. Rev. Monte Ellis (otherwise known as Akashan), a minister of the Spiritual and Divine Science Church in Los Angeles, predicted that "the area around Santa Monica, California, will be jarred by an earthquake at the beginning of the year."

On February 9, 1971, the predicted earthquake hit the San

Fernando Valley, a part of Los Angeles County not far from the coastal town of Santa Monica. An odd thing about the prediction had been that Santa Monica is not on the San Andreas Fault, nor is the San Fernando Valley. The epicenter of the earthquake, about eighty-five miles away from the San Andreas Fault, was in a region that had not been geologically active since the Ice Age some 10,000 years ago. Registering 6.5 on the Richter scale, the quake caused considerable damage and a loss of sixty-two lives. Most of the casualties were in a Veterans Administration Hospital in Sylmar, in the Valley, and faulty construction of the hospital's wings may have been the major cause of death. The earthquake jarred also the sensibilities of Californians, especially children who were traumatized by the experience, including the aftershocks, and had to have special psychiatric care to lessen their fears.

As April 1972 approached, San Francisco's prophets of earthquake once again became active. This year April 22 was the date most favored in the Earthquake Sweepstakes for the Big Quake. I sent in my entry to San Francisco's Mayor Alioto for May 22, but emphasized that any quake would be less serious than the 1971 Los Angeles quake. Experimenting with a synchronistic system for arriving at precise times and dates, I predicted that "it will be of a strength between 3.5 and 3.6 on the Richter scale and that it will happen at approximately 8:18 P.M. New York time, or 5:18 P.M. San Francisco time."

Either my method doesn't work, or I got the wrong year.

Panic about California's fate has provoked a semischolarly book published in late 1972 by Peter Briggs. Its title is *Will California Really Fall into the Sea?* (David McKay, 1972). As one reviewer put it, "Nifty title—but the answer is: No, not for another sixty million years." Briggs, however, warns that San Francisco and Los Angeles are overdue for the Big Quake that could be far more serious than the 1906 earthquake and fire in San Francisco.

In its December 1972 issue *Psychic* magazine published a prediction by Dr. Reuben Greenspan that San Francisco would experience an earthquake on January 4, 1973, with a Richter magnitude of between 5.9 and 6.2 (slightly less than the February 1971 Los Angeles earthquake). When informed of this prediction, Dr. Charles Richter, originator of the earthquake scale, termed Dr. Greenspan "a fool and a charlatan."

San Franciscans became agitated about this prediction, which was widely publicized. Many people planned to be out of town on the fateful date of January 4. News of the panic spread. *The New York Times* reported on it, demoting *Dr.* Greenspan to *Mr.* and calling him a "recluse." Finally, on December 29, at a conference in Palo Alto, Greenspan recanted: "It gives me profound pleasure to announce that the prediction I made two years ago that an earthquake would take place is not correct." An arithmetical error had been made. Greenspan added that he would make no more earthquake predictions.

Greenspan claimed his predictions were not psychic but were based on equations of the gravitational pull of the sun, moon, and Jupiter. When the moon and Jupiter were in conjunction—both pulling from the same direction—the combined attraction would set off a quake when passing over an earthquake-prone fault.

At least one San Franciscan was unperturbed by Greenspan's announcement of the impending earthquake. In an unusual press release dated December 25 from the Gold Mountain Monastery on Fifteenth Street, it was revealed that the Venerable Master Tu Lun Shuan Hua would not permit the earth to quake as long as he was in San Francisco. Four years earlier, Christmas Day 1968, the master had said to his disciples: "It is not that there can't be an earthquake but rather that I will not *permit* the earth to quake. I don't want to move into the ocean, and I don't want my disciples, or anyone else, to move there either."

As the press release (entitled "An Unbelievable News Announcement") stated, "Every year the Master has made the same announcement: 'I will not permit the earth to quake,' and to this day the big earthquake hasn't happened."

An additional news release on December 27, 1972, gave the reasons for this confidence:

> For those little acquainted with the Master's inconceivable and beneficent powers and the responses resulting from his rigorous practices and magnanimous virtue, a situation which prevailed in Hong Kong from 1950 to 1960 may be cited. When the Master arrived in Hong Kong the city was constantly threatened and often struck by typhoons. At that time the Master said that as long as he remained in Hong Kong the city would be safe from the disasters of wind, and that this would hold true while he was living in the city, but that after he left he would pay no attention to the problem. Strangely enough, during the years of his sojourn in Hong Kong the city remained untouched by big winds. Time and again hurricane warnings alarmed the city but each time the storm either died out or changed course. The immunity of the city was dramatically evident when on some occasions the storms beat a straight course for the city only to suddenly veer off as close as 15 miles from shore.
>
> In 1960 the Master left Hong Kong and went to Australia. During that year upon his absence from the city, Hong Kong was hit by the worst typhoon in years which did vast amounts of damage.
>
> Coincidence you say? Yet isn't it strange how year after year the calculations keep indicating earth disturbances due in the San Francisco area and year after year the city remains solid and peaceful! "I can't handle big business," says the Old Master, "but I can cope with little things like earthquakes."

We are glad that someone can. Although San Franciscans were amused by this news, at another level they are not prepared to take needless chances. The Old Master is welcome to stay in San Francisco for the rest of his days.

"San Francisco—The City That Waits to Die" is the quaint phrase used by the BBC in a television special on the dangers awaiting that city from earthquake. Records from previous years of earthquakes occurring in California were run through a computer with a visual television display. They happened just about everywhere except San Francisco, where the San Andreas Fault is locked. When it goes, the energy released will be enormously destructive, worse than the 1906 quake. In their dramatic way, the BBC were very successful in scaring the hell out of San Francisco.

The earthquake that devastated Managua, Nicaragua, also dramatized the possible destruction awaiting San Francisco. Earthquakes in Mexico, Pennsylvania, Southern California, Northern California (Eureka) also got page-one coverage in the *San Francisco Chronicle*. An office building was being abandoned because it was not earthquake-proof. Measures were being taken to relocate school buildings away from the San Andreas Fault. San Francisco is earthquake conscious.

What sort of effect did the publication of Greenspan's earthquake prophecy have on the Central Premonitions Registry? People started writing in with *their* premonitions that an earthquake would occur on January 4. One man even wrote in a list of some 300 cities with a prediction that they would suffer earthquakes that year. If he were right with one, he apparently thought, then he would win the Earthquake Sweepstakes.

By now, every Californian has given thought to the possibility of dangerous earthquakes along the San Andreas Fault. "When?" is the question uppermost in mind.

Once this seed idea has been widely planted, then organizations like the Central Premonitions Registry can no longer put any credence into premonitions, whether hunches or dreams, that predict such an earthquake. If by contrast, residents of

New York City began in large numbers to have dreams of disastrous earthquakes, then the situation would be very different. New York is far less likely geologically to suffer earthquakes and fear of such earthquakes among New Yorkers is correspondingly rare. Thus it would be more likely that a rash of earthquake dreams from New Yorkers might be precognitive rather than caused by present fears.

If dreams and visions are to have any value as prophecy, then the percipients must not know of earlier prophecies, which might have influenced them. For it is only completely independent prophecies that can be fitted together to make any kind of dependable larger picture of the future.

Most premonitions, such as those from dreams, generally relate to the percipient's own future. But the future of large-scale events is glimpsed only fragmentarily, and then usually limited to the percipient's own involvement in that event.

The prophecies of Edgar Cayce relating to earth changes came to him while he was in trance. For the most part these prophecies related to years long after his death, from the period 1958 to 1998 and even to 2001. So far, nothing of a startling nature—no great earth changes—have fulfilled his prophecies. Some Cayce interpreters have argued that since Cayce was often right in his clairvoyant medical diagnoses, then, therefore, he must be right about his prophecies of world destruction. "It's all from the same bottle," Jess Stearn told me.

But it would *not* seem to be from the same source at all. Cayce's medical diagnoses seemed to tap a body of medical knowledge that can be roughly identified with medical practices and theories of his day and just before. His prophecies, however, came in the context of life readings, generally about someone's former life in Atlantis. Although reincarnation has its believers and disbelievers, as does Atlantis, only Atlantis could be easily subject to proof or disproof. If we had incontrovertible evidence of a historical Atlantis that was destroyed about 11,500 B.C., then we might well feel that Cayce's prophecies were to be taken as seriously as his history.

When asked in 1936 if Los Angeles would be safe, Cayce replied: "Los Angeles, San Francisco, most all of these will be among those that will be destroyed before New York even."

Naturally, people often asked Cayce exactly when this would happen. His reply prophesied that others would give this information: "As to times, as to seasons, as to places, *alone* is it given to those who have named the Name—and who bear the mark of those of His calling and His election in their bodies. To them it shall be given."

One of Edgar Cayce's sons, Hugh Lynn Cayce, said recently that his father never gave any dates on upheavals in California, despite all the rumors. "We deplore the use of these prophecies for sensationalism or doomsday predictions. Unfortunately, many people do pick this kind of thing out of the mass of other information and play or dwell on it out of proportion. . . . Trying to piece the readings together to come up with specific dates is impossible." [1]

Scarcely a month goes by without some prophet somewhere having picked it as his entry in the Earthquake Sweepstakes. My first choice had been in the latter half of May, around May 22. "As to the year," I wrote the Central Premonitions Registry in 1969, "I'm not sure. . . . When an earthquake there does happen, I do *not* believe that California will fall into the sea as some have predicted; and indeed there will be more earthquakes later."

Whereas most earthquake scientists have logically concluded that any earthquake in San Francisco would have to be enormously destructive—because of the pent-up energy in the locked San Andreas Fault—my August 1971 dream tells me otherwise: that houses sway, not collapse. There may well be a destructive earthquake in about twenty years, but by then it is very likely that a scientific early-warning system will have been developed to minimize loss of life. Already many scientists are working on such an early-warning system, and it is only a matter of time before they put earthquake prophets out of business.

What would be my reaction if indeed I do manage to witness an earthquake in California as I have dreamed? I suspect it might be similar to that of the psychologist William James, who left Cambridge to go to Stanford University early in 1906. A Cambridge student named Blakewell said to James before he left, "I hope they'll treat you to a little bit of an earthquake while you're there. It's a pity you shouldn't have that local experience."

On the morning of April 18, when he was lying in bed awake at about 5:30, the room began to sway, and James said: "Here's Blakewell's earthquake, after all."

James later described it as reaching

> fortissimo in less than half a minute, and the room was shaken like a rat by a terrier, with the most vicious expression you can possibly imagine, it was to my mind absolutely an *entity* that had been waiting all this time holding back its activity, but at last saying, "Now, *go* it!" and it was impossible not to conceive it as animated by a will, so vicious was the temper displayed—everything *down*, in the room, that could go down . . . and the shaking so rapid and vehement. All the while no fear, only admiration for the way a wooden house could prove its elasticity, and glee over the vividness of the manner in which such an "abstract idea" as "earthquake" could verify itself into sensible reality. In a couple of minutes everybody was in the street, and then we saw, what I hadn't suspected in my room, the extent of the damage. Wooden houses almost all intact, but every chimney down but one or two,

and the higher University buildings largely piles of ruins. Gabble and babble, till at last automobiles brought the dreadful news from San Francisco.

James wrote his relatives that "this experience only rubs in what I have always known, that in battles, sieges and other great calamities, the pathos and agony is in general solely felt by those at a distance; and although physical pain is suffered most by its immediate victims, those at the *scene of action* have no *sentimental* suffering whatever. Everyone in San Francisco seemed in a good hearty frame of mind; there was work for every moment of the day and a kind of uplift in the sense of a 'common lot' that took away the sense of loneliness."

James discovered the bravery and closeness of human beings in time of calamity. Although the abstract idea of earthquake may evoke fear, the reality of earthquake may signal the operation of reserves of courage and resourcefulness. While not everyone might experience "glee" as did James when he felt the abstract become real—the archetype become reality—I cannot doubt that San Francisco will prove tougher than nature.

11

Prophecies of Apollo

The Apollo missions to the moon represent a fulfillment of prophecy. It may be synchronistic that the name Apollo, the ancient Greek god of prophecy, was chosen for a program that fulfilled in detail the predictions of Jules Verne a century before in his novel *From the Earth to the Moon*. Verne described a spaceship launching from Florida that carried three men to the moon in approximately the same time that it actually took a century later.

Prophecy tends to be self-fulfilling. Neil Armstrong, the first man on the moon, spoke for the *Apollo 11* crew on the reasons they chose the name *Columbia* for their command module: "Columbia was . . . a national symbol, but more important the choice was an attempt to reflect the sense of adventure and exploration and seriousness with which Columbus undertook his assignment in 1492. And, of course, there was a tie-in with the Jules Verne exploration book that turned out to be, in some ways at least, an accurate prediction of the technique and details of the *Apollo 11* flight." Jules Verne's spaceship had been named the *Columbiad*.

I don't know when Neil Armstrong first read Verne's novel, but I suspect it may have been when he was a teenager in Ohio. Certainly that is when I read the book and every other science-fiction book I could find on space travel. My very first attempt at writing, in the eighth grade, was about a voyage to the moon. When I graduated from Central High School in Akron, Ohio, in 1954 I listed my "life ambition" in our yearbook "to be the first man on the moon." I received a lot of joshing about that ambition—not because it was *I* who wanted to go to the moon—but because going to the moon was impossible. Years later I became convinced that the most important explorations man could undertake were into inner space; but I never lost my fascination with voyages to the moon.

My first attempt to use the Apollo mission as a focus for prophecy showed more about the nature of precognition than it did about *Apollo 12*. I meditated on November 12, 1969, to see if I could get impressions about the next flight to the moon. I sent this prediction to the Central Premonitions Registry: "While meditating today on the upcoming flight of *Apollo 12* to the moon, I got the impression that there is a grave danger for this flight. Unless something in the fuel system or electrical system is corrected, there will be an explosion which could kill the astronauts. It may be that this flight will be aborted, for I do not feel these astronauts will reach the moon."

The *Apollo 12* mission went without mishap, but the next mission, *Apollo 13*, fulfilled the prediction in such detail that this seems to be displacement—hitting on the next target instead of the one being concentrated on, a common phenomenon in parapsychological experiments.

A few hours after launching on March 13, 1970, *Apollo 13* had an explosion in the oxygen tank of a fuel-cell system. The world joined in prayer for the safe return of the three men in a ship that had lost most of its electrical power and that had to bypass the moon without landing in order to return to earth. The flight was aborted.

The meditation image that gave rise to my prediction contained both words and symbols. I saw an image of the spaceship and sensed that an explosion was imminent. The words *fuel system* and *electrical system* came to mind. I then asked myself if the astronauts would land on the moon. I saw an image of the famous photograph of the first footprint made on the moon by Armstrong, but then it was crossed out with a large X. I felt this meant the astronauts would not land on the moon.

Later, after *Apollo 13* returned, NASA published a report which indicated that the oxygen tank that short-circuited had been dropped about an inch at the assembly factory in October 1968. Thus the defect giving rise to the explosion was in existence at the time of my meditation, perhaps giving rise to my premonition.

But on April 14, 1970, when the president called for universal prayer for the three men in the endangered craft, I too was concerned. I joined in the prayer and then meditated on whether they would return safely. I had the following image, which I filed with the Central Premonitions Registry: "They will return safely and get a tremendous heroes' welcome. I had an image of them being showered with confetti and, oddly, the astronauts were holding flags or banners. It may be that a photo in the press will depict them like that."

More than two weeks later, May 2, *The New York Times* published a photograph of two of the astronauts being welcomed in Chicago with a ticker-tape parade. Confetti and streamers showered the happy astronauts, and positioned above them were two American flags. But in my meditation image they were holding flags. When I cut out the photo for my records, I glanced back to reread the story. There, above the caption "Astronauts Hailed in Chicago" was now another photo showing through from another page. It depicted several young men at a protest in New Haven. They were holding flags. My meditation image seems to have combined the two photos seen in quick succession, much in the same way as dreams condense images.

On November 10, 1970, I meditated on the next flight, *Apollo 14*. I filed with the Central Premonitions Registry this prediction: "The *Apollo 14* flight scheduled for January 31, 1971, will be successful. The landing on the moon may be a bit rough, though. Some unusual rocks may be found in a crater or on a crater's slope. During the time of *Apollo 14*'s flight, there may be a headline something like 'Three Fliers Released.'"

The *Apollo 14* was, of course, successful. The only "roughness" with the landing was a malfunction of radar just prior to the command module's landing. One rock on a crater's slope did seem of unusual interest. As stated in *The New York Times* of February 13, 1971: "Of greatest interest to the scientists was an ash-white rock fragment that Captain Shepard and Commander Mitchell chipped off a boulder near the rim of Cone crater. . . . It was one of several whitish rocks the astronauts saw that scientists believe may be remnants of the moon's original crust."

A newspaper connection between the *Apollo 14* flight and the release of fliers seemed to be fulfilled on March 9, 1971, when *The New York Times* ran a front-page story of four American airmen being released by Turkish kidnappers. On the same page was an article about the *Apollo 14*'s New York parade. That part of the prediction came true four months after the initial meditation.

More than a year before, on April 24, 1970, a young parapsychologist friend tried his hand at giving me a psychic reading. One prediction seemed so unlikely that I registered it with the Central Premonitions Registry: ". . . that within three months I would be going to Texas. I have neither the money nor the inclination to do that, nor any reason to, so if it should come true, it will be very interesting." My friend also predicted that I would have some dealings with someone in public relations, which, while not startling, was certainly not a usual sort of thing in my life then.

It turned out that the two predictions were related, though the fulfillment came a year and three months later, in July 1971. *Psychic* magazine flew me to Houston, Texas, to visit the Manned Spacecraft Center for an interview with *Apollo 14* astronaut Edgar Mitchell. I had to go through the Manned Spacecraft Center's public relations officer, and this entailed a number of long-distance phone calls. It was worth it. At last I was able to approximate my boyhood dream by entering the mock-up Apollo lunar module that surveyed a mock-up moon at the Manned Spacecraft Center. But more important, I was able to get from Captain Mitchell the details of his dramatic moon-earth ESP experiment that gave significant evidence that ESP could penetrate not only the vastness of space but also the limits of time. Because of a delay in the lift-off of *Apollo 14*, the periods scheduled for the astronauts' rest times (and Mitchell's ESP transmission times) were also delayed; the percipients on earth, however, recorded their guesses at the old prearranged times, thus making their guesses before Mitchell had himself determined the target order—ergo, precognition.

Mitchell's ESP experiment from *Apollo 14* was only the first step of a more comprehensive plan to bring to parapsychology the brains and money it needs to effect a major change in consciousness. After his retirement from the U. S. Navy and from NASA in October 1972, Mitchell formed a new organization called Edgar Mitchell and Associates (EDMA) whose specific objectives are:

> 1. To help bring science's understanding of the nonphysical aspects of the universe to the same level as its knowledge of the physical aspects.

2. To help bring that knowledge to society through the media and other channels, and through the application of research findings in useful goods and services.

3. To help society recognize that a transformation of human consciousness from egoism toward selflessness is necessary for planetary survival.

4. To demonstrate that people can awaken in themselves a state of higher, universal consciousness which will operate in every aspect of life.

In short, we hope to direct the course of history away from its present catastrophic trend of ever-greater global crises.[1]

Mitchell's beginning explorations into the realms of inner space, which include the establishment of a Noetics Institute for the study of consciousness, have the potential, it seems to me, to bring mankind vaster benefits than the Apollo program itself. Other astronauts may not share his vision, but they respect his intellect. As *Apollo* 7 astronaut Walt Cunningham said about Mitchell in a recent interview: "Now Ed's something else. . . . I tend to pooh-pooh what he's doing. But one thing has me worried: Ed's no dummy."[2]

Mitchell once made the statement that he would not run his life by psychic predictions since we know too litttle about the way ESP functions. My mental retort was that I, too, would not run my life by psychic predictions—but because I know too much about it. Not only errors of psychic perception make reliance on predictions hazardous in some cases, but the apparent pliability of the future necessarily limits prophetic accuracy. The case in point might be the flight on *Apollo 16*.

On March 31, 1972, I received a strong impression that the upcoming flight of *Apollo 16* was in grave danger from a leaky cylinder that could explode on the firing of the third stage. Shortly afterward a leaky hose on the *Apollo 16* was replaced. The only cylinder that exploded did so after the flight's return; and several people were injured, though no one was killed. Had this explosion happened in space, the results most likely would have been fatal.

Was a potential disaster scaled down to a mishap? Or was I simply in error? There is simply no way of telling for certain. But if prayers have anything to do with it, then it may be that a potential disaster was avoided.

I had sent my premonition to Edgar Mitchell, who was at that time on the back-up team of *Apollo 16*. When we met in Chicago in May 1972, he told me that he had received a number of premonitions about the flight. Fortunately, they too proved to be wrong. Mitchell assured me that NASA made every conceivable check and double check to ensure that nothing could go wrong. And yet, I thought, had they not made such a check before *Apollo 13?*

There is always a human factor in every machine made by man. And there always exists that remote possibility of the human factor introducing error. Yet, if our minds can exert any influence over events—and I think they can—then it may be that prophecies of doom exert a self-fulfilling tendency just as prayers may exert a positive direction of self-fulfillment. Especially on the personal level can positive prophecy bring its own fulfillment.

As I mulled over the implications of *Apollo 16* for prophecy, during a stay in Chicago for a Spiritual Frontiers Fellowship convention on May 17, 1972, I received a telephone call from a New York reporter who interviewed me about my predictions of the Apollo missions. I told her about the meditation image I had during the crisis of *Apollo 13* that was fulfilled later when I saw a photo of the astronauts being welcomed by a ticker-tape parade in Chicago. As I hung up the telephone, I heard the noise of bands playing in the distance. I left the hotel to walk a block away to see what the parade was for. There were the *Apollo 16* astronauts being given another ticker-tape parade in Chicago—this time in my own reality instead of a newspaper photo. Synchronistically, both *Apollo 13* and *Apollo 16* flights, of which I had had premonitions, projected their pattern of triumph to the same place. Once more the wheel of destiny seemed to have come to rest, fulfilling the positive prophecies of Apollo.

The astronauts of *Apollo 17* made the last flight to the moon scheduled for this century. To the disappointment of many workers in the space agency and allied aerospace fields, no other manned space missions are being planned to visit other planets. Yet immediate prospects for cooperation with the Soviet Union in the 1975 Skylab project are encouraging. Talks over the last two years have finally led to a cooperative agreement to join forces in space explorations.

I anticipated this American-Soviet cooperative effort in a meditation image on February 2, 1969. While meditating on the moon, I saw the flags of the United States and the Soviet Union plant themselves almost simultaneously on the moon. Like snakes, the two flags intertwined themselves and grew into an olive tree. The olive tree bore first strange sparkling fruits like Christmas tree decorations. Then the tree bore olives, which when ripe, fell to Earth where hungry fishes devoured them.

I sent my interpretation of this image to the Central Premonitions Registry with the following predictions: "The space exploration efforts of the Russians and Americans will be united. From this union of common effort will come a peace between America and Russia. There will be some spectacular gains, probably scientific, that will come early after the united program."

The symbolism of the olives feeding the hungry fishes suggests a peace that will bring sustenance to the spiritually hungry. By 1980 I anticipate this spiritual renaissance to blossom forth—somehow a gift from the sky.

What will be the future of manned spaceflight? I still hold

to my prediction published in May 1971 that "the United States and Russia will join forces to explore the outer planets." [3] Although no such programs are on any drawing boards now, I think they will be by the late 1970s. The discovery of a new propulsion system for space travel will revolutionize our current concepts of rocket ships. No longer will tons of liquid fuel have to be ignited to thrust a rocket from its launching pad. Far more sophisticated systems will utilize an entirely new principle that will enable spaceships to attain velocities far beyond anything we have today. Technology makes leaps in quantum jumps, from the horse to the steam engine, from automobiles to airplanes, from rocket ships to . . .

12

2001: Armageddon or Age of Aquarius?

Ultimately the source of Western Civilization's most influential prophecies can be traced back to the Bible. The Old Testament prophets were regarded as speaking the word of God, generally in the context that people must heed His word or a dire fate awaited them. No dates were given for prophesied catastrophes, though, of course, a Messiah was promised. In the New Testament, prophecies of the return of Jesus were believed by people of that time to apply to their own age. But as the centuries passed, prophets chose the year 999 or 1000 A.D. as the time of "the End," Jesus' second coming, and, naturally, "The Millennium." As the millennium approached, countless more prophets joined their voices to proclaim the imminent doomsday.

Apparently reprieved—for the new millennium came without disaster—prophets next took the date of the second millennium, 2000 A.D., as the time of "the End." There were, of course, many prophets in between who looked forward to Judgment Day in their own time. The British Museum Library has hundreds of prophetic interpretations of the Bible published in the last few centuries. The Book of Revelations, especially, has been interpreted many hundreds of times with many hundreds of different dates for "the End." Indeed, I would judge that speculating on the meaning of biblical prophecies must have been one of the most popular pastimes in past centuries. These speculations left their mark.

It was in such a prophetic tradition that the following manuscript was alleged to have been written by a Polish monk in 1790. The sixth edition, which I photocopied, was published in Leipzig (in German) in 1848, and here follows the first translation into English of his prophecies for the twentieth century.

So remarkable has each century of the world been, so will moreover the twentieth century be the most remarkable of all; and I already see in the spirit of it all the fate and destiny which will befall the inhabitants of the earth at the time. All, which may be considered appalling and terrible, will befall the human race in this century. By the beginning of the year 1900 in many countries the princes will revolt against their fathers, the citizens against their government, children against their parents, and the whole human race against each other.

So it will last until the year 1938, when a universal war in the whole world in which man against man will be intent only on death, will draw all creation into destruction. Devastation and destruction will overtake whole countries; desolate, empty of people, and destroyed will be the greatest and most respected cities.

In the year 1986 once again peace will be established; it will be only a few years. . . .

In 1988 a terrible comet will appear in the heavens and by a cruel blow on the earth will raise the water from the seas and drown whole lands.

In 1996 a universal earthquake will shake the whole earth, and all Italy, Naples, Sicily, Portugal, and Spain will vanish forever into the ground.

Finally there comes in the year 2000 the last day of the Lord, on which he judges the living and the dead. Stars and comets will fall from the heavens and set the earth on fire with lightning; and so will this earth pass, which stood for 6,000 years since the creation.

The history of the world goes on—wonderful for the righteous and terrible for the sinners. Judge of the world, have mercy on all. . . .[1]

Although the Polish monk was off a million or so years in his estimate of how long man has been on earth, his prophecy that 1938 would see a "universal war" seems uncomfortably close for a shot in the dark. Especially since he was aiming from 1790, allegedly. At least we know that the prophecy was in print by 1848. Even, in a telescopic way, his description of the early part of the twentieth century seems to characterize political and military strife that led to both World War I and II.

The monk's prophecy of a comet (meteor?) striking the earth in 1988 compares interestingly with Jeane Dixon's prophecy that in the 1980s "something literally earth-shaking will occur, a natural phenomenon . . . something like a meteor. It will . . . involve the shifting of the waters of the earth." And, by now, the theme of "universal earthquake" has become familiar in prophecy.

The monk's prophecy that the earth would be bombarded from the heavens and set fire to in the year 2000 reflects, certainly, the biblical prophecy "For behold, the day cometh, that shall burn as an oven."

By comparison, Nostradamus gives us only one date for the twentieth century: "In the year 1999 and seven months, from the sky shall come a great king of terror. . . ." As usual, Nostradamus spoke in riddles, but this is more explicit than most of his prophecies: something (or someone) coming from the sky in July 1999. In the centuries since Nostradamus wrote that prophecy, many interpreters have proposed various meanings for the quatrain, but the date of 1999 remained as a year for extraordinary events.

In the late nineteenth century an occult group flourished in England but drew their inspiration for prophecy from the Great Pyramid of Egypt. The pyramidologists treated the Great Pyramid as a symbolic prophecy in stone. Relating the architecture of the Pyramid to prophecies of the Bible, they arrived at the year 2001 as the last date on their prophetic calendar. ". . . in September, 2001, mankind, pyramidologists believe, will have reached another stage in its growth, another civilization—perhaps a theocratic world-state—and all things will be made new." [2]

These prophetic traditions left their mark on the prophecies of Edgar Cayce and those who consulted him. One questioner, apparently versed in the occult, asked Cayce in 1936, "What great change or the beginning of what change, if any, is to take place in the earth in the year 2000 to 2001 A.D.?" Answered the entranced Cayce, "When there is a shifting of the poles. Or a new cycle begins."

Cayce seemed to link his earth-change predictions for the years 1958–1998 with the "day of the Lord," saying, "That as has been promised through the prophets and the sages of old, the time—and half time—has been and is being fulfilled *in this day and generation*, and that soon there will appear in the earth that one through whom many will be called to meet those that are preparing the way for His day in the earth. . . ."

Many years later Jeane Dixon prophesied that a child born on February 5, 1962, would become a great religious leader whose power would grow greatly until 1999. At least, that was the initial interpretation of her symbolic vision; later, she changed the child to an antichrist. Mrs. Dixon also prophesied that 1999 would issue in a time of world holocaust to be followed by an era of peace. The year that Nostradamus singled out of the twentieth century—1999—maintains its prophetic power.

I first read Nostradamus's prophecy on December 10, 1965, when I was working as a science editor for a book publisher. I pondered over the meaning of his strange image: a king of terror coming from the sky. One interpreter thought this predicted interplanetary warfare. The next day I went to a nearby bookshop to try to find another book on Nostradamus that would give other interpretations. It was not in stock, but as I was leaving the bookshop my eye caught an absurdly titled book on a sale table: *My Contact with Flying Saucers*, by Dino Kraspedon (mentioned in Chapter 9). I opened the book to a prophecy that (synchronistically) supplied an interpretation of Nostradamus's 1999 prophecy: Toward the end of this century, another sun would enter our solar system and form a binary star system with our own sun. It would not emit light until it reached our solar system. The orbits of the planets would be changed such that Mercury would move into the area between the present orbits of Venus and Earth, and Venus would move further out beyond earth. The Earth, in turn, would assume a new orbit where the planetoids are now. "The Earth will begin its new millennium with a new source of light to illuminate it. . . . The Sun which is to come will be called the Sun of Justice. Its appearance in the heavens will be the warning signal of the coming of the One who will shine even more than the Sun itself."

Nothing could have struck me as being more fantastic, especially since the prophecy was attributed to the captain of a flying saucer from one of Jupiter's moons. Intellectually, I rejected the whole book as fantastic nonsense. But some strikingly peculiar events made me think again. I took a nap after reading the book and awoke to a strange sight: A miniature sun, its surface swirling as if it were alive, first appeared on the wall and then floated in the air about a foot away. I rubbed my eyes and opened them again. It was still there.

The visionary (?) sun vanished as I went to answer a knock on the door. The wife of an artist friend invited me to a party at their home that evening. When I arrived, the first thing that caught my eye was a painting of a sun in a blackened landscape.

"What on earth does it mean?" I asked my friend.

"The end of the world," he replied. "I just finished painting it today."

I then told him about my vision of a sun. "That's a coincidence," he said. "I had a vision today too. I saw lights on the wall for about five minutes." He drew me a picture of the nine lights he had seen. I wondered if his visionary lights somehow would put mine in perspective. I checked his drawing carefully with star maps of the heavens. Only one area coincided with the lights, except that his vision showed one additional light in the constellation of Monoceros, or the Unicorn. Monoceros is located near Sirius, the Dog Star.

The drawing may, of course, have been somewhat inaccurate. Yet it did seem to single out some "dark" star near Sirius. My attention was further drawn to Sirius the next morning in the office when I discovered a magazine, *Sky and Telescope*, that our company librarian had strangely decided to send me. It contained an article on Sirius and its binary companion, jocularly called Pup since it is the Dog Star's companion. Pup, I learned, is a white dwarf star of about the same mass as our sun and makes an orbit around Sirius every 50.09 years. Located 8.7 light years away, Pup can be seen only when it is the farthest distance away from the main star, which will happen in 1973. A peculiarity of white dwarfs like Pup is that they become eventually dark stars, emitting no visible light when their matter becomes "degenerate." Astronomers have now identified a number of dark (invisible) stars by radio astronomy.

Could it be possible that one of these dark stars is even now heading toward our solar system? I'm certain that astronomers to a man would regard the idea as sheer nonsense. Intellectually, I do too. But the synchronistic pattern begun by my search for a meaning to Nostradamus's 1999 prophecy makes me wonder if somehow, some celestial body from outer space is on its way.

If such a thing did occur, it would neatly explain some otherwise puzzling prophecies of Nostradamus:

> The moon shall be obscured in the deepest darkness,
> Her brother shall pass being of a ferruginous [blood-red] color;
> The great one long hidden under the shadows,
> Shall make his iron lukewarm in the bloody rain.

That one seems to say that when the moon and the sun are eclipsed, then another celestial body will become visibly red. Another of his prophecies is more specific: "The great star shall burn for the space of seven days,/A cloud shall make two suns appear. . . ."

Again and again Nostradamus refers to a great eclipse of the sun which would happen just before the "great conflagration." (Having an additional sun might indeed give rise to the day that shall burn as an oven.)

Nostradamus says that "when the eclipse of the sun shall be at noon day, the monster shall be seen . . ." and elsewhere refers to an eclipse to be seen in France. The next total eclipse of the sun in the neighborhood of Paris will happen on August 11, 1999.

The Old Testament concludes with a prophecy by Malachi that links the conflagration with a "Sun of Righteousness." "For, behold, the day cometh that shall burn as an oven. . . . But unto you that fear my name shall the Sun of Righteousness arise with healing in his wings. . . ." The prophet of a new Messiah is apparently referred to by Malachi when he adds: "Behold, I will send you Elijah the prophet before the coming of the great and dreadful day of the Lord."

Presumably Jews might regard this new prophet as signalling their Messiah, while Christians might regard him as announcing the second coming of Christ. The prophet Elijah was said to have been reincarnated in John the Baptist, who proclaimed Jesus as the Messiah.

If indeed a new sun came into our solar system, whether called the Sun of Righteousness or the Sun of Justice, it would inspire sufficient awe to create a whole new religious order (among the survivors). I cannot help but wonder if this may be connected with the symbolic vision that Jeane Dixon had on February 5, 1962. Her vision began with a brilliant sun from whose rays stepped forth Ikhnaton and Nefertiti with a child that was offered to the world. Within the sun Joseph guided the others like a puppeteer. Rays of light emanated from the child to blend with the sun and blank out Ikhnaton. Nefertiti, stooping to drink from a water jug, was stabbed in the back and vanished. Grown to manhood, the child was adored by all races and religions as a cross above him spread about the world.

Historically, Ikhnaton was the first monotheist, symbolizing the one God by the solar disk. Some scholars, such as Sigmund Freud, suggest that Moses was influenced by Ikhnaton's tradition. Nefertiti at the water jug may symbolize the Age of Aquarius, usually depicted as a woman with a water jug. Her being stabbed may mean that the Aquarian Age will be ushered in by violence. Joseph, famous as a dream interpreter for the Pharaoh, might symbolize the new prophet. The cross obviously symbolizes Christianity. While Mrs. Dixon interpreted this vision to mean that the child would be a descendant of Ikhnaton and Nefertiti, I think it more likely refers to the resurgence of the symbol of the sun for a single God, which last happened in Ikhnaton's reign.

Mrs. Dixon's surprising turnabout in her interpretation of this vision—first, the child was to be the new Messiah; later, to be the antichrist—may be related to an earlier vision of a serpent with wisdom in its eyes. Mrs. Dixon now feels that he represented Satan, as the serpent in the Garden of Eden. But the serpent has many other symbolic meanings. For instance, the symbol of the medical profession is a winged staff about which two serpents intertwine, a symbol of healing that goes back to the ancient Greeks. The serpent also symbolizes Kundalini, the spiritual power that rises up the spine. A combination of the sun and the winged staff symbols might explain the otherwise perplexing image given by Malachi: "The Sun of Righteousness with healing in his wings."

Perhaps such a symbol might be used by some new Messiah of a neo-Christian religion one day, inspired by the appearance of a new sun.

Perhaps related to such a cosmic event is a prophecy given in trance by a talented Texas psychic, Ray Stanford. His book *Fatima Prophecy* [3] presents several readings on the meaning of the strange events witnessed at Fatima in 1916. Stanford said, "At the present time (March 3, 1972), the physical solar system heads in space at a great rate toward a mass of cosmic energy and particles which, in the *not-distant* future, will collide with the sun and planets and energize the ionosphere of planets and the atmosphere, and will energize the photosphere of the sun—unless it is averted."

The spinning sun that was seen by thousands of people at Fatima represents to Stanford "a symbolic prophecy of what could happen to the sun. The three times of spinning and then ceasing symbolize three days. The 'sun's' darkness, compared to the normal sun, symbolizes that the sun shall be darkened. The rays of light symbolize that strange and diverse energies shall come from the sun and shower the Earth. The finally coming closer symbolizes that, in the final phase, the sun will emit energies that would change the Earth drastically. . . ."

Stanford says further that the sun is already changing magnetic poles, and that three days of darkness will fulfill the biblical prophecy that "the sun shall be darkened and the moon shall not give forth her light."

Stanford also prophesied on March 3, 1972, that by May 16 a miracle would occur at Garabandal, Spain. After the miracle, there would be left a sign, above the pines of Garabandal, that would "be related to the sword and yet unto the cross, and will be a symbol of devotion to the overcoming of 'the forces of darkness.' "

This unusual prophecy seemed to be fulfilled (a few days late) in May 1972, as reported by the *National Enquirer* (September 10, 1972). A group of forty British tourists visiting Garabandal, the site of reported appearances of the Virgin Mary eleven years before, said that they saw the sun whirling and going up and down. Mrs. Gwendoline Hurndall, a nurse at St. Joseph's Hospital in London, described her experience:

> At about 6:45 one evening during our visit, we had gone to a clump of *pines above the village* to pray, when I heard cries of "Look at the sun!" I looked up and found I could stare straight at the sun without sunglasses. Part of the outline of *a cross* was just vanishing from the sun as I looked up. Then the sun began to spin like a wheel, first one way and then the other. Then it jumped up and down like a yo-yo for a few minutes before starting to spin again.
>
> And while all this was happening, different colors were emerging and receding all around it—pink, yellow, blue, grey. This went on for about half an hour. Then some of us decided to pray again, and just as we knelt, the sun divided itself into two parts. A central part stood forward from the rest and moved toward us like a huge Host, a sacred communion wafer.

Others in the group also testified to seeing the spinning sun. Jenny Deefholt, a retired secretary, said that "the sun was like a white, spinning disk. Suddenly I saw Our Lord's face appear in the center of the disk. Then it disappeared, and the sun started to dance in the sky."

Father Alec Barilone, a London priest, added: "I definitely saw the sun spinning very fast—first clockwise, and then counterclockwise, surrounded by all sorts of colors. I believe it was a miraculous manifestation."

And I wonder if this vision of the sun might predict a new Messiah whose symbol will be a new sun.

Already, tens of thousands of evangelical Christians think that the Second Coming of Christ is imminent. As Edward B. Fiske noted in *The New York Times* (October 8, 1972):

> They cite recent events in the Middle East as fulfillment of Biblical predictions and note that this time around even some secular thinkers—notably the pessimistic wing of the ecology movement—are talking the language of doomsday.
>
> Most of the speculation is based on three events described in the Bible as the immediate forerunners of the Second Coming:
>
> —The return of the Jews from exile to occupy the land of Israel.
>
> —The unification of Jerusalem under Jewish rule.
>
> —The rebuilding of the Temple.
>
> By anyone's scoresheet, it is now two down and one to go. . . . Daniel 7 talks of the formation of a 10-nation confederacy; some see this fulfilled in the Common Market. . . . Others see the fulfillment of the prophecy from Isaiah in the problem of urban sprawl ("Woe unto them who join house to house, who lay field to field, till there is no place"—5:8) and in the rise of women's lib ("As for my people, children are their oppressors, and women rule over them"—3:12).

Since biblical prophecies contain no dates, they cannot be evaluated in any scientific way. Yet they cannot be disregarded either when such specific predictions as the return of the Jews and the unification of Jerusalem are fulfilled. Just what influence the biblical prophecies may have had on the Jewish nation was suggested by the American psychiatrist and parapsychologist Jan Ehrenwald in a talk given in Jerusalem a few years ago: "Isaiah's message of the Messianic Days to come kept alive the hope of scores of generations of the children of Israel that 'the remnant shall return' and that the people who 'walked in darkness' would see the light, and that 'the light will shine upon those who dwell in the land of the shadow of death.'

"I don't have to remind an audience gathered close to the site on which these prophetic words were uttered to what extent their power has contributed to the ensuing historic events that led to the Zionist movement and culminated in the founding of the Jewish state." [4]

The self-fulfilling prophecy of Isaiah demonstrates the extraordinary power of an idea when charged with faith and hope. The "effective myth" becomes reality more than 2,000 years later.

One wonders, too, if the Battle of Armaggedon will be self-fulfilling. Here is an edited prophecy by Cheiro (Count Louis Hamon) from *Cheiro's World Prophecies* (London: Herbert Jenkins, 1931):

> . . . the Armageddon yet to come will be brought about by the return of Judah and Israel to their country. . . . As the ancient boundaries of Palestine originally extended to "the river of Egypt," so will the Israelites with their co-workers in Palestine open up Egypt. . . . This development will arouse antagonism from the followers of Islam, and Turkey [Egypt?], backed by Russia, will endeavor to recapture Palestine.
>
> In this coming war which is by no means far off, England will be attacked in all her Mohammedan possessions. She will give India her freedom, but religious warfare will rend that

country from end to end until it becomes equally divided between the Mohammedan and the followers of Buddha. . . . Italy and Germany will at the same period be at war with France, and Spain under a Dictator will be engaged in a life and death struggle in North Africa. . . . The United States will be engaged in war with . . . Japan and will not take part until later in the European carnage. . . . In Ireland there will be Civil War between the North and South. . . . This coming War although far greater and more terrible than the last, will be only one of the many that will occur in the next few hundred years leading up to the final Armageddon.

As foreshadowed in Ezekiel, chapter xxxviii, the great battle of Armageddon will be fought on the plains of Palestine . . . this conflict will be a life and death struggle for the contending armies fighting in Palestine. It describes that the people of the North, by which Russia is evidently indicated, will descend into that country. . . .

At first the prophet indicates that the people from the North are likely to be successful; he then proceeds to describe how the Lord of Hosts will come to the aid of His people by earthquake, storm, flood, fire and plague. . . .

In prophesying the Aquarian Age, Cheiro predicted that a great leader of men would appear, a Jew who "will in the end dominate Russia." About religion, he said that "in the next hundred years there will be as many religious sects in the World as there are pieces of the supposed 'true cross' in existence at the present time.

"In the coming years, great evangelical 'revivals' will sweep through all countries, side by side with Anarchy, Atheism, and Free Thought of every kind. Civilisation will chameleon-like change its colour to suit each new wave of thought, and Chaos will drive her chariot of destruction through fields of Peace into the avenues of War."

And then Cheiro prophesied the meaning of Armegeddon to the Aquarian Age: "It is only War in the end that will save humanity. It is only when the world will be satiated with blood, destruction, and violence, that it will wake from its present nightmare of madness—and thus it is that the coming 'War of Wars' fits into the design of things.

"Through intense tribulation shall man be brought nearer to perfection and more fitted to enjoy the wonders of the new Aquarian Age, that, born in blood and sacrifice, will in the end fulfill the meaning of its symbol 'the Water Bearer' whose pouring out of water on the earth is the emblem of un-selfishness—the negation of Self—arrived at through suffering."

Cheiro's prophecy seems to have hit on an extraordinary number of major events of the last thirty years. The present situation in the Middle East was only too clearly described by him: Russia aiding Arabs to take back Egyptian territory captured by the Israelis. Is the stage set for Armageddon? If so, it may not be so far in the future as Cheiro thought.

As to a major effect of the Age of Aquarius, Cheiro prophe-sied that "women have to come to the front in all matters of public life. I have no hesitation in saying that there is no body of men who will be able for long to resist the tide of thought that for good or evil is bringing women into power." It would seem, then, that Women's Liberation will indeed be successful.

If Cheiro is correct that the bloodbaths of war are necessary to awaken the human race to a new age of understanding— then the years ahead will not be easy ones. It is probable that the biblical prophecy of Armageddon is overdramatized in the same way as the story of Noah and the flood was over-dramatized. The Great Flood covered not the world but only a portion of the Near East in the Tigris-Euphrates area. The Old Testament prophets were concerned mainly with the fate of their own people, the Jews, and their prophecies should be viewed accordingly as applying mostly to Israel.

While scarcely anyone today confidently thinks the Age of Wars is over, many fear nuclear holocaust from use of hydrogen and atomic bombs. I feel, however, that man will finally be successful in outlawing nuclear weapons. But when will the Age of Wars end? I feel that mankind, when confronted with nature's even more terrible catastrophes, will finally realize the madness of acting out the archetype of war.

Jung once remarked that shortly before the Second World War, many of his patients dreamed about Wotan, the god of war. This symbol of war presaged the enactment of the archetype of war, a collective pattern that has persisted through all ages. Once the archetype was initiated, Jung said, we "become possessed by it—and forced to its fatal conclusion."

13

Of Time and Tomorrow

> The fact that the future can be occasionally foreseen does not exclude freedom in general, but only in this particular case. Freedom could become doubtful only if everything could be foreseen.
>
> —C. G. Jung

How much freedom of choice do we have? Is tomorrow already waiting for us, completely preformed in our inner "blueprint" of life? Or can we alter the "blueprint" before it becomes a reality?

Those are questions that could be answered only by trying to foresee as much of "everything" as possible. Sometimes the choices seem already made by some inner destiny. Here is an unpleasant example.

Once at a party I was goaded into giving the hostess a psychic reading. I tried to avoid it, since party atmospheres can easily overload me emotionally when I'm in a psychic state, but she insisted. I did something I hope I never do again —I dropped my censor against giving negative information that could not help a person. I told her that she would soon lose her job, that she would never marry the man with whom she was going, and that she would die a violent death. Soon after she lost her job. And within a year and a half she fell twelve stories from a window in an attempt to escape a rapist.

I only recently learned that a sensitive in Maine claimed to establish contact with the woman's spirit and that part of the message was "Alan Vaughan was right." But I had been picking up her future from her inner self.

Coincidentally, at the time of her death (but before I learned of it) I had a dream that symbolically indicated that she was "suffering for Christ." That suggests to me that, in her inner self, she accepted death in much the same way as Robert Kennedy—as a fulfillment of an archetypal role she had chosen to play.

Here is an example, however, of someone who chose not to play a role. In a reading I gave to a New York actor, I told him that he would be going to Hollywood to act in Western films and that eventually he would settle in the West. A few months later he got an offer from a famous Hollywood director of Western films who offered to fly him to Hollywood for a screen test for the lead of his next Western. The actor didn't go. Apparently his "blueprint" of life could be altered by his freedom of choice. Whether he chose wisely or not is quite another question.

In the dream records of Christine Mylius and myself, key events of life appear in dreams often years in advance, woven in an intricate web of time with major and minor themes that are repeated with variations. These individual patterns of life that I call individual archetypes surpass in complexity the fugues of Bach and together make up a person's "blueprint" of life, which in turn is part of a larger pattern.

An analogy might be made with blueprints for a house. Each room might be considered analogous with an individual archetype. Every house has a kitchen, bathroom, bedroom, and so on, though the arrangement of them is different in every blueprint. The way the rooms are to be furnished would be analogous to the individual's own arena of choice. In some cases, the individual might be able to alter the blueprint if he found it did not suit him; but once the builders have begun to construct the house, making alterations becomes very expensive. The archetypal roles, once activated, tend toward completion.

Some people move into prefabricated houses, giving little thought of designing things to suit themselves. Their choices are made all at once.

The group of houses together make up a community that interacts on a higher level. The communities form cities, the cities form states, the states form countries, and so on, to the complete universe. The people living in houses may think that these arrangements are at random. But if someone flies overhead in an airplane, he can quickly spot the highly organized patterns of human habitation. After seeing one town from the air, he might be able to predict what the next town will look like.

In the same way, from the vantage point of another dimension, the sensitive can see the patterns of life, if only through a keyhole.

The analogy breaks down in one important point: life is not a static group of houses but a dynamic arena where archetypes struggle for supremacy. The arena is named Time, and the winner gets Tomorrow.

Groups of people seem to be drawn into common plans of action, each person's inner "blueprint" dovetailing with that of the others in a synchronistic way that achieves a result greater than any one of them by himself could have accomplished. While a person may think chance coincidence is the cause for his becoming involved in this activity, the overall plan is highly organized, and that person has a place in it.

An analogy might be in the formation of complex organic molecules. The individual atoms do not hook up together at random, but in highly organized patterns that draw the atoms together in precise arrangements. Our bodies are made up of countless such molecules, each one in turn part of a higher structure. If human beings were part of a cosmic plan so vast that by comparison a hydrogen atom in the toe would be as a human to the planet earth, then the human being would have no conception of his individual role in that vast organism. Very likely even the "toe" would not know about the "nose." Yet there would be an ultimate consciousness that would have awareness of all its parts.

Even as our bodies are composed of incredibly complex units of organized life—planned in microscopic DNA molecules—so perhaps does society have its own "blueprint" that tends toward higher complexity, that continues evolution on a societal level. More and more complex units become capable of greater and greater action. The groups interact—they battle —and give birth to new and higher orders of groups. Society evolves.

The evolution of society is very much like the development of a human being. It builds on past patterns (archetypes). History repeats itself, but with variations. The United States, for instance, repeats patterns from antiquity, drawing upon a different archetype for each stage of development. Like Carthage, which was a colony of the sea-going Phoenicians, America fought a war for independence and outgrew the sea-going British in importance. Like Rome, America rejected the idea of monarchy and established a republic that included a large confederacy of states. Like Rome, America has been attacked and drawn into wars from which she has emerged victorious and that have enlarged her sphere of influence. Like Rome, America is eager to establish worldwide peace through establishing peace-keeping armies throughout the world. Like Rome, signs of decadence are beginning to develop in America. Rome debased her coinage; America devalued its dollar. The American eagle, like the Roman eagle, has begun to lose its prestige.

Can such a comparison have any predictive value? Here are some prophecies for America based on the archetype of Roman civilization:

• The American president will acquire greater and greater power.

• The Senate and the House of Representatives will correspondingly lose power, being demoted to the status of yesmen.

• The government will become increasingly corrupt and resort to dubious methods to maintain control.

• Semimilitary organizations at the capital (like the Roman Praetorian Guard) will increase in power such that eventually they will control the presidency.

• Eastern culture will heavily influence American thought in the years to come. Eastern cults and religions will gain strength here and finally supplant traditional Christianity. A new religion will combine Eastern and Christian concepts.

• Americans will become less concerned with individual freedom and more concerned with security. Guaranteed incomes and ever more lavish television spectaculars will correspond to "bread and circuses."

• America's technology will rise to new heights.

• Armies will shrink in size. Americans will no longer be drafted (already a virtual certainty). Foreign nationals will be employed in peace-keeping operations.

• America will become more and more dependent on importing goods from other countries.

• The percentage of affluent Americans will continue to grow, as will their decadent excesses. Yet an influential minority will continue to fight to maintain older standards.

• A clash with the "barbarians" (probably Russians) will

weaken America but put it into alliance with Russia. In fact, the clash may already have happened, being dubbed the Cold War, the Korean Police Action, and Vietnam. The alliance with the Soviet Union should follow soon, but with America in a weaker position than now.

• A *Pax Americana*—a period of relative lack of war—should be soon upon us. Optimism should run high, decadence should run wild, and the stage will be set for America to begin a search for new spiritual values.

So that is the basic scenario using the pattern of ancient Rome as the model. The reader can probably supply many more predictions from classical history. Of course the Roman empire lasted for 2,000 years, while America is only 200 years old. The pace of life accelerates continually.

If America can be compared with Rome, Britain, of course, can be compared with Athens (and often has been). Britain would now seem to be in the stage that Athens experienced when it lost its colonies but retained its wisdom as "the university of the world." Its military power has dimmed, its economy has suffered, but it maintains supremacy as the font of philosophy. Will some modern British philosopher take the role of Aristotle as tutor to some future world conqueror on the order of Alexander? Will some Oxford-educated African prince seek to unite all Africa into a nation of conquerors? The ancient archetypal roles of life will seek expression again.

How are these archetypal patterns transmitted to individuals? Jung has postulated the existence of a collective unconscious from which archetypes arise spontaneously. But I would go much further in tracing the psychic heritage of man and postulate a dual heredity, a psychic counterpart to physical heredity. When a child is conceived, his biological future already preexists in a physical "blueprint" contained in DNA structures. This physical "blueprint" recapitulates all of man's evolution as the fetus goes through stages where it has gills and a tail and finally emerges in nine months as a human baby. Not only does the child develop from collective patterns of its biological ancestors, but it has its own unique pattern, influenced most heavily by its direct parents. The chromosomes battle for supremacy in establishing the child's biological "blueprint." The color of eyes from mother, musical talent from father, physical height from mother, hair from father. The laws of genetics are well known. By studying a child's parents and grandparents, one can skillfully predict when a child will mature, when (or if) he will go bald, whether or not his teeth will need dental work, and so on. Even personality can be in some part predictable, such as disposition, temper, extraversion or introversion, although it is not clear how much close association with parents might influence that.

Yet many children baffle their parents when it comes to more subtle characteristics—characteristics of the mind, which broadly might be termed *psychic*. A clue that these psychic or spiritual qualities might also be inherited lies in the fact that sensitives are able to read this psychic "blueprint" to predict the future. Perhaps the theological concept of a spirit entering the fetus or child could be of use in explaining this apparent dual heritage. The spirit, in the view of reincarnationists, carries with it memories of past lives—like so many beads on a string. The British sensitive Joan Grant, for instance, says she can recall more than forty lives, and has written novels about a number of them, including *Winged Pharaoh* about a life as an Egyptian pharaoh's daughter who became a coregent of Egypt. Edgar Cayce "recalled" a life as an Egyptian priest named Ra-Ta who was later deified as the great god Ra. This strikes me as fanciful when compared with history. Why is it, one wonders, that "past lives" so often come from colorful periods of history when the persons were important or rubbing shoulders with the great?

How many Cleopatras, Napoleons, Caesars, Christs can there be?

If, however, this spiritual consciousness—this psychic "blueprint" of life—were formed in a way analogous to our physical "blueprints" of life, then it might explain this paradox. If we have spiritual ancestors as well as genetic ancestors, then we might be drawing upon the memory patterns (or archetypes, if they are sufficiently old) of famous people in the past. We might exhibit psychic or spiritual characteristics of these spiritual ancestors in the same way we exhibit physical characteristics of our physical ancestors. If we look like grandfather, we don't say, "I was grandfather in a past life." That is absurd, since grandfather was alive when we were born. Yet, certainly, one might well be heavily influenced in his physical makeup by grandfather, as might the other grandchildren.

If the analogy of physical genetics goes further, then perhaps the spiritual archetypes battle each other for supremacy in the way that chromosomes vie for position. For every positive archetype, there seems to be a negative one. For every Christ, there seems to be an antichrist. For every Roosevelt, a Hitler. Even the youngest philosopher can see that "nobody's perfect." We are the product of both positive and negative forces.

So, instead of the "beads on a string" philosophy of reincarnation, I would postulate as a more general pattern the idea of archetypal roles from the past contributing to our spiritual makeup in a way analogous to our physical ancestry. It would explain why so many people "recall" lives of famous persons, or even why so many schizophrenics think they have become some famous person. They mistake the inherited spiritual memory for a reality; they become so identified with this archetype from the past that they lose their own identity.

It is perfectly possible, of course, that this spiritual heredity is strongly influenced by belief or desire of a culture. In India, where reincarnation is viewed as a karmic pattern of life, there have been many documented cases of children recalling a past life, generally of someone who died shortly before they were born. But the previous personality usually was not connected with the present family. Among the Tlingit Indians in Alaska, where reincarnation is viewed as a continuation of the family, children sometimes recall past lives of ancestors of their family and may even exhibit distinguishing birthmarks that offer evidence for their memory. As the reincarnation researcher Dr. Ian Stevenson of the University of Virginia Parapsychology Division has pointed out, cultural beliefs seem to condition the actual occurrences of memories of past lives in children.

Americans, probably more than any other people, represent an amalgamation of many nations and cultures. Americans who recall past lives (generally through hypnotic regression) seem to reflect this variety, though most of the claimed memories are beyond verification. Edgar Cayce's trance readings of past lives also seem to describe mainly famous periods of history, including problematical ones, such as Atlantis. A few of his readings of past lives have been documented with evidence that there *was* such a past personality, though these tend to be the unglamorous type. Occasionally Cayce would be called on to read the past lives of an infant and to predict the infant's future. In one case, he predicted that an infant boy would become a great doctor of the mind. The boy's father wanted him to go into business but indeed the boy went to Harvard Medical School to become a successful psychiatrist. Cayce's reading was apparently based on a psychic "blueprint" of life, which in turn was based on "past lives." Of course, my question would be: Were these actual "past lives" through which a personality had gone? Or was Cayce picking up impressions of the strongest archetypes from the past that made up the boy's psychic "blueprint" of life? Perhaps someday reincarnation research will come into the laboratory so that we can find the answers.

In the meanwhile, though, it seems to me that an individual is born with a psychic "blueprint" that contains the basic patterns of his future and that is based on patterns from the past—on the building blocks of psychic life—that I term *archetypes*. Put another way, a person as a spiritual entity makes his basic choices for the future before he is born. He enters the world with his inner destiny.

This inner destiny or "blueprint" seems to be chosen so as to fit in a complex interlocking weave of a hierarchy of society's "blueprints." An analogy might be seen in experimental drama. The overall play is written by a single author; the roles are written so as to interact with each other toward a certain dramatic climax. Yet there is a certain amount of freedom for the actors who try out for the roles. They may be able to alter certain scenes or their precise words so as to fit better their own personalities. The playwright might write them a new scene if he thinks they can perform it to the greater benefit of the drama. Other scenes may be cut or rewritten, depending in part on the actors available. Theater is often a fluid experiment. Yet the basic structure of the play is fixed. The ending is rarely changed by rewriting, though it does sometimes happen. The characters (the archetypal roles) are basically set. Yet sometimes especially good actors will be able to add to their roles once they have demonstrated their capability. More often, the actor's brilliance is demonstrated by how *well* he plays the role, not how he changes it.

In his lifetime an actor will play many roles. So perhaps do we all play out many archetypal roles in our lives, trying out continually for new plays to form a new society.

Many people, especially the young, may not know what

their capabilities are. They may not know what their inner "blueprints" want to guide them to. They may not know what choices to make, what roles to try out for.

The value of prophecy is in showing what possibilities these archetypal roles might offer if given expression in life. Prophecy can show the alternate scenarios of life and their consequences. And up to a point—within the framework of our inner "blueprints"—we can choose which of our possible futures we want to become reality. If we, like John and Robert Kennedy, choose to play the role of the hero, then we should understand that heroes must die.

It has been my experience that generally prophecies are ignored. Indeed, that seems to be part of the archetypal role of the prophet as exemplified by Tiresias or Cassandra. The prophet is rebuffed by people who do not pay any attention to his predictions, and then when (or if) they are fulfilled, he plays the unpopular role of saying, "I told you so." Even more annoying, the prophet seldom can tell a person exactly what to do to avoid some calamity (perhaps because the calamity is already in a final "blueprint" stage and cannot be changed). Since the natural function of extrasensory perception is to warn, like an early-warning radar system, few prophets go beyond this stage. However, the precognitive faculty can be trained to pick up other future situations as well; and it is in the positive directions that prophecy can be of most use. But only if a person is willing to take the prophecy to heart. And the prophecies that we take most to heart are those we make ourselves.

When people consult psychic sensitives, they generally are not interested in experiments or in a delineation of their past lives or their future, or what they happen to be thinking at the moment. No, it is usually very practical: "I have a problem. What should I do?" Most of the problems are the same ones that people go to psychiatrists or counselors for:

emotional upsets, broken loves, work frustrations, and a general feeling that something is not going right. Life has become a burden instead of a joy. Life has become so complex that a person does not understand it. A person is not getting out of life what he feels he should be. The person, in a word, is unhappy. He feels that someone else might be able to tell him how to become happy, how to solve his problem, tell him what choice to make.

When I am faced with such a person, I find that before long I am asking him if he recalls any dreams. And by eliciting his associations and identifying symbols, I help the person interpret the dream so that he gets the message from his inner self. Sometimes the dreams seem to point to future events. But my interpretation is only as valid as the impression it makes on the dreamer: if he becomes convinced that his inner self does have a higher knowledge and that dreams can express this wisdom such that he can rationally understand it, he will likely take to heart his own advice.

I believe that the main reason for unhappiness is a dissonance between a person's inner "blueprint" and the life he is actually leading. And that happiness is, by definition, a fulfilling of one's potentialities—a complete expression of one's inner "blueprint." If you are doing well at what you came into this world to do, then you are happy.

Most people are not aware of being psychic, nor do they usually have intellectual awareness of their future (or their future possibilities). Yet each of us does possess a guiding inner "blueprint" that can be tapped. I have found meditation particularly helpful in establishing such a contact—of releasing the mind from the grip of logic so that it can merge with the far-wiser inner self. Sometimes the meditation will yield actual images and words that will guide me. But more often I feel only a sense of oneness with my complete self and find that quite unconsciously I do the right thing to solve any problem I might have. By becoming more intuitive, by learning to trust gut feelings, one can become self-fulfilling.

Very probably there is a very good reason for our not being intellectually aware of our inner "blueprints." Our conscious minds would quickly crack under the strain of trying to make the enormous number of decisions for every little action that is necessary for our lives. Most of our decisions that we consider rational really are not. They spring from the inner self, and we merely embroider them with rationality, to give them the appearance of logic at work. Our friends can generally detect this rationalization with which we so cleverly disguise our words and actions, but if they are true friends, they will not condemn us; for they know they do the same thing.

If we *did* have to contend in our conscious minds with all these decisions, we would be a complete wreck in a short time. Imagine, for instance, the analogous way we run our bodies. If we had to remember to breathe, and to make our hearts beat, and to make our muscles work one by one, we probably would not survive more than a few minutes. We would forget something essential. Instead, we give the body general orders and the details are carried out by subsidiary elements of which we have no consciousness.

Perhaps, in a similar way, as Edgar Cayce said, "Mind is the builder." Here I read the word "Mind" to be something considerably more in scope than "what is on your mind at the moment"; I view the Mind as the greater consciousness that incorporates the superconscious and that directs psychic energies.

A visual demonstration of how this works has been given by Dr. Thelma Moss in experiments at UCLA's Neuropsychiatric Institute. When a number of healers or "green thumb"-type people tried to heal injured plant leaves—which were being photographed by radiation field (Kirlian) photography—the leaves' energy fields began to show the typical colors and appearance of healthy leaves. One successful healer described his technique: "I try to get into a trance state. I fill my mind with happy thoughts of a bright, green, healthy leaf. I try to visualize a flow of energy from my fingertips to the leaf's surface. At first the good results startled me, but now I'm aware of what I'm doing. I even seem to have some control over it." [1]

Mind is not only the builder, but also the healer. An older way of expressing Cayce's sentiment is more familiar: "Prayer changes things."

And what of time and tomorrow? Which archetypal patterns of life, both individual and societal, will win the favor of expression in reality? It may depend on which images of life we hold in our minds, which futures our minds will build, which things our prayers will change.

"In the beginning was the word, and the word was with God, and the word was God." The "word" or *logos*—the culmination of all archetypes—preexists in a timeless dimension, and when transformed by divine energy becomes at one with a divine reality. In a microcosmic way, each human being shares in that divinity with his own psychic energy. The archetypes of his inner "blueprint" become transformed by that divinity into his reality. Each of us participates in the cosmos, a cocreator with God. By developing our individual "blueprints" of life to their highest achievement, we come closest not only to individual fulfillment but also fulfillment of a higher order of destiny.

To those who would seek to find their place in the cosmos, I recommend the shortest of prayers: "Thy will be done. May my will be Thine."

To those who see no evidence of God in their lives, I recommend that they explore their own patterns of prophecy.

Notes

CHAPTER 1

1. F. Nicol, "Apparent Spontaneous Precognition: A Review," *International Journal of Parapsychology* (1966).

2. I. Stevenson, "Precognition of Disasters," Journal *ASPR* 64, no. 2 (1970): 206.

3. H. F. Saltmarsh, *Foreknowledge* (London: G. Bell & Sons, 1938), p. 11.

4. C. Honorton, "The Automated Forced-Choice Precognition Tests with a 'Sensitive,'" Journal *ASPR* 65, no. 4 (1971): 476–81.

5. *See* Chapter 14, "Dreaming on Things to Come," in Ullman and Krippner with Vaughan, *Dream Telepathy* (New York: Macmillan, 1973).

CHAPTER 2

1. C. G. Jung, *Letters*, vol. 1 (Princeton: Princeton University Press, 1973), p. 395.

2. C. G Jung, *Archetypes and the Collective Unconscious*, 2nd ed. (Princeton: Princeton University Press, 1968), p. 79.

3. A. Hardy, *The Living Stream* (London: 1965), p. 242; quoted in Koestler, *Roots of Coincidence* (New York: Random House, 1972).

4. R. G. Stanford, "Psi in Everyday Life," *ASPR Newsletter*, no. 16 (Winter 1973).

CHAPTER 3

1. This chapter is adapted from a paper delivered at the November 1972 meeting of the Society for the Investigation of Recurring Events, New York Academy of Sciences, New York, N. Y.

2. S. Krippner, "The Cycle in Deaths Among U.S. Presidents Elected at Twenty-Year Intervals," *International Journal of Parapsychology* 9 (September 1967): 145–53.

3. See Chapter 4 for an attempt to cope with that dilemma, the Central Premonitions Registry.

CHAPTER 4

1. H. Greenhouse, *Premonitions: A Leap into the Future* (New York: Geis, 1972).

2. *National Enquirer*, May 23, 1971.

3. *Revue Metapsychique* (1930): 50–2; quoted by E. Bozzano, *Discarnate Influence in Human Life* (London: International Institute for Psychical Research), pp. 204–7.

4. Cheiro, *Confessions* (London: 1932), p. 167.

CHAPTER 5

1. E. Osty, *Supernormal Faculties in Man* (London: Methuen, 1923; reprinted New Hyde Park, N. Y.: University Books, 1971).

CHAPTER 6

1. E. J. Garrett, *Adventures in the Supernormal* (New York: Garrett Publications, 1949), p. 19.

2. E. R. Dodds, "Supernormal Phenomena in Classical Antiquity," S.P.R. *Proceedings* (March 1971): 194.

3. J. C. Barker, *Scared to Death* (New York: Dell, 1969), p. 140.

4. Quoted in E. Osty, *Supernormal Faculties in Man* (London: Methuen, 1923), pp. 111–2.

5. "Parapsychological Association, 14th Annual Convention (1971)" *Journal of Parapsychology* (December 1971): 313–4.

CHAPTER 7

1. W. H. C. Tenhaeff, "Depth-Psychological Background of Spontaneous Paragnostic Experiences," *Proceedings of the Parapsychological Institute of the State University of Utrecht*, no. 3 (January 1965): 22–4.

2. H. Bender, "The Gotenhafen Case of Correspondence Between Dreams and Future Events," *International Journal of Neuropsychiatry* 2, no. 5 (1966): 398–407. Documentary film, *Der Fall Gotenhafen*, 48 min., sound, 16 mm., Institut für den Wissenschaftlichen Film, Nonnenstieg 72, Göttingen, W. Germany.

3. H. Bender, "Parapsychology in Germany," Parapsychology Review 3, no. 5 (September-October 1972): 12.

CHAPTER 8

1. *Light* 86 (1966): 60–72.

2. J. Sherwood, *The Fourfold Vision* (London: Spearman, 1965), pp. 151–2.

3. A. Vaughan, "The Phenomena of Uri Geller," *Psychic* (June 1973).

CHAPTER 9

1. *Time*, February 25, 1966, p. 102.

2. E. E. Cayce, *Edgar Cayce on Atlantis* (New York: Hawthorn, 1963).

3. R. H. Saunders (ed.), *Health: Its Recovery and Maintenance*, by Abduhl Latif (London: Rider, 1928), pp. 270–8.

CHAPTER 10

1. H. L. Cayce, interview, *Psychic* (September 1972): 10.

CHAPTER 11

1. E. D. Mitchell, "An Adventure in Consciousness," *Psychic* (December 1972): 23.

2. H. Muson, "Comedown from the Moon—What Has Happened to the Astronauts," *New York Times Magazine* (December 3, 1972): 142.

3. *National Enquirer*, May 23, 1971.

CHAPTER 12

1. *Höchst Merkwürdige Prophezeiungen eines alten Mönches in*

Polen [Highly remarkable prophecies of an old monk in Poland] (Leipzig: Julius Koffka, 1848), pp. 43–4.

2. H. J. Forman, *The Story of Prophecy* (London: Cassell, 1936), p. 73.

3. Published in 1972 by the Association for the Understanding of Man, P.O. Box 5310, Austin, Texas 78763. Price: $6.95.

4. J. Ehrenwald, "Precognition, Prophecy, and Self-fulfillment in Greco-Roman, Hebrew, and Aztec Antiquity," *International Journal of Parapsychology* (December 1967): 230.

CHAPTER 13

1. D. Hudson, "Injured Plant Leaves Can Be Cured by Psychic Healing, Scientist Claims," *National Enquirer*, March 25, 1973.

Index